Transforming Your Church

Seven Strategic Shifts to Help You Successfully Navigate the 21st Century

Mark Conner

Sovereign World

Sovereign World Ltd.
PO Box 777
Tonbridge
Kent TN11 0ZS
England

Unless otherwise stated, all Scripture quotations are from the Holy Bible,
New International Version, copyright © 1973, 1978, 1984 by
International Bible Society. Used by permission.

ISBN 1 85240 272 5

The publishers aim to produce books which will help to extend and
build up the Kingdom of God. We do not necessarily agree with every
view expressed by the author, or with every interpretation of Scripture
expressed. We expect each reader to make his/her judgement in the
light of their own understanding of God's Word and in an attitude of
Christian love and fellowship.

This Sovereign World book is distributed in North America by Renew
Books, a ministry of Gospel Light, Ventura, California, USA. For a free
catalog of resources from Renew Books/Gospel Light, please contact your
Christian supplier or call 1-800-4-GOSPEL.

This Sovereign World book is distributed in Australia/New Zealand by
WCF Distributors, a ministry of Waverley Christian Fellowship,
1248 High St. Rd. Wantirna South, Victoria, Australia
(*Tel*: 613 9871 8300 *Fax*: 613 9801 6926 *Email*: books@wcf.org.au).

Typeset by CRB Associates, Norwich
Printed in the United States of America by Versa Press Inc.

'Mark Conner is one of the up and coming choice leaders in the church of the 21st century. His heritage is rich and his pastoral ministry is graced with wisdom and spiritual discernment. He is a man to be trusted in the coming years.'   **Frank Damazio**
Senior Pastor, City Bible Church

'If you have a desire to hear what the Spirit is now saying to the churches, you can find no better starting place than Mark Conner's *Transforming Your Church*. This book has the potential to lift you to new levels of effectiveness that you might never have dreamed possible!'   **C. Peter Wagner**
Chancellor, Wagner Leadership Institute

'This book is an outstanding tool for every church leader who is serious about seeing growth and fruitfulness in their ministry . . . the practical insights will challenge and inspire any believer who longs to be a part of building what Jesus said He would build: His Church!'
Brian Houston – *Senior Pastor, Hills Christian Life Centre*

'Mark Conner is a gifted pastor and communicator. It is wisdom for every church leader to consistently evaluate where their church is at and what they are doing. Mark gives some key areas to look at and insightful suggestions to facilitate change.'   **Dick Iverson**
President, Ministers Fellowship International

'Of all the books on leadership I've read, none is more sensible and helpful, because Mark outlines a clear-headed, practical, step-by-step process of leading your church through change. Read it. Use it with the people on your leadership team.'   **Gary Kinnaman**
Senior Pastor, Word of Grace Church

Mark Conner's book is a real 21st century handbook for the new paradigms that God is bringing into the new millennium Church. I highly recommend it.'   **Dr Emanuele Cannistraci**
Senior Pastor, Evangel Christian Fellowship

'Mark Conner is an outstanding leader who pastors a remarkable church. Both are well on their way to making a great impact for God in the nation of Australia and beyond.'   **Dr Stuart Robinson**
Senior Pastor, Crossway Baptist Church

'In this excellent book, Mark Conner has nailed the strategic shifts essential for a church to keep from 'spilling' the revival and harvest coming in the 21st century. Don't miss a point as you go over your ministry and ask yourself the serious questions of change.'
Larry Stockstill – *Senior Pastor, Bethany World Prayer Center*

Acknowledgements

I am reminded of two sobering facts as I write this book. Firstly, the Bible tells us that there is nothing new under the sun (Ecclesiastes 1:9–10). Secondly, what does any of us have that we haven't received (1 Corinthians 4:7). The following people have greatly impacted my life and their influence is evident throughout the pages of this book.

I would like to thank...

My wonderful wife, Nicole, who is my best friend and my biggest encouragement and also my children, Josiah, Ashley and Natasha who are the joy of my life.

My parents, Kevin and Joyce Conner, for their constant love and godly example and for giving my sister Sharon, and me, a love for God and His church.

Those who influenced my life, beginning in my teenage years – Richard Holland, Dick Iverson, Steve Powlison, Wendell Smith, Ken Wilde, Ken Malmin, Mike Herron, Emanuele Cannistraci and Frank Damazio.

The other outstanding church leaders who have influenced my life and ministry in recent years – Brian Houston, Bill Hybels, John Maxwell, Phil Pringle, Larry Stockstill, Casey Treat and many others.

The wonderful staff, leaders and congregation of Waverley Christian Fellowship who have given me the opportunity to grow and provided much encouragement along the way. You have given me far more than I could ever give to you.

The Lord Jesus Christ for choosing me to be His child and for giving me the privilege of serving Him.

Contents

Foreword

Mark Conner is one of the finest young leaders I know. He is that rare combination of a bright mind and a fully yielded heart. His observations concerning the shifts that must take place in order for a church to reach its redemptive potential are profound. And Mark's insights are far more than theory. One visit to Waverley Christian Fellowship is all it will take to turn cynics into believers. The Church for the 21st Century will require a higher level of leadership than any other era in human history. Books like this one will contribute a great deal to the development of such leadership.

I am deeply grateful to Mark for his friendship and the impact that he is having on churches and leaders in Australia, and increasingly all over the world.

Bill Hybels
Senior Pastor
Willow Creek Community Church

Introduction

I am a preacher's kid, or a PK, as some people like to call us. Actually, my dad always called me a 'TO' which stands for 'theological offspring'.

Anyway, I've grown up in church and I've loved every minute of it. Growing up as a PK was actually a lot of fun. Sure, there were the occasional unrealistic expectations from people in the church for me to be perfect, but my parents were patient and they encouraged me along the way. We met a lot of wonderful people and visited some fantastic places. Best of all, my parents lived what they preached, so serving God was the only way to go for me.

Early on in my life I made a choice to live for God. In my teenage years I confirmed that commitment and began to develop my own personal relationship with God.

My parents never pressured me to be in full-time church work or to be a preacher. Instead, they encouraged me to develop my own abilities and dreams. As it has turned out, after a brief stint as a printer, I ended up on full-time church staff and have been so for over twelve years. I have had involvement in youth ministry, worship ministry, administration and now as a Senior Minister.

When I took over the senior leadership role of our wonderful congregation, Waverley Christian Fellowship, in 1995, I determined to do it to the best of my ability. I love the church and I'm committed to making it all God wants it to be.

The task is overwhelming at times and way beyond my natural ability. That's why I have invested a lot of time in prayer, reading and talking with other leaders to learn all I can to help me lead our local church with excellence and the power of the Holy Spirit.

In 1996, I attended a conference in California hosted by Peter Wagner on the New Apostolic Reformation church. This conference brought together a wide variety of Christian ministries from around the world for fellowship, sharing and interaction. During this conference, I noted certain aspects common to churches that are flourishing and effective.

As a result of my observations, I felt the Lord quicken to me seven **Strategic Shifts** that are taking place in the Church today. I needed to be aware of these and flow with them.

Over the last four years, I have focused on making these shifts in my own life and in our local congregation. It has taken time and we still have a long way to go, but I have seen incredible blessing from the Lord as we have committed ourselves to get in step with what He is doing.

The purpose of this book is to share these **Strategic Shifts** with you so that you can receive a greater understanding of what God is doing in our generation. There has never been a more significant time than right now for the Church to rise up and take up the challenge. I believe that this book can help you to transform your church!

God bless you.

Mark Conner
April 2000

God's Master Project

God's Master Project

Do you ever think about heaven? Have you ever wondered, 'What is God doing today and is His desk as messy as mine?' Well, one thing we know for sure, God is very busy working on one major project. It's the focal point of His time and energy and He's very passionate about it. Which project? The Church, of course.

Almost 2000 years ago, Jesus said that He would build His Church (Matthew 16:18–19). The Church isn't just some side issue or something God is doing to amuse Himself until the world ends. It's at the very center of His heart and it consumes His thinking.

Yes, God is aware of the rise and fall of governments, the economy, the environment and the sharemarket. But His focus of attention is on one thing – the Church of Jesus Christ. It's on the top of His 'To Do' list and it's the main topic of conversation in heaven's throne room.

The Church has been and is central to His entire purposes since the beginning of time (Ephesians 3:10–11). He has an awesome plan and He's working right now to see it accomplished. The Church is God's master project.

What is the Church? [1]

Let's take a minute to talk about this entity called the 'Church'. First of all, let's recognise what the Church is **not**.

1. **The Church is not a building.** Jesus is not focusing His attention on the latest trends in modern day architecture or on a material building made of bricks and mortar.

2. **The Church is not one particular denomination.** The Church is not just the Baptists, the Catholics, the Pentecostals or some other particular Christian group. It's not based on some specific tradition, doctrine, emphasis or structure.

3. **The Church is not one particular nationalistic group.** Jesus doesn't just love Australians, Americans, Jews or any other particular nationality. You don't have to be born in a certain country to be a part of the Church.

So what is the Church? The definition of this word emerges out of the Greek culture of Jesus' time. The word 'Church' literally referred to a group of people called out of their homes to gather together for an important meeting in the city. Applying this spiritually, we see that the Church is God's people from every nation 'called out' of the kingdom of darkness and translated through new birth into the kingdom of God. It is God's people assembled together to meet with Him and accomplish His purpose.

There is only one true Church around the world today. It is made up of every person who has been truly born again through repentance and faith in Jesus Christ, regardless of race, gender, social status or denomination. The one true Church is made up of many local churches. Believers gather together in different places around the world to worship Jesus, love one another and reach their community for Christ.

The Destiny of the Church

Okay, so God is working on the Church. It is very important to Him. But what is the Church going to look like, anyway? How will we know when it has reached its destiny? Thankfully, the Bible gives us some clues as to what the Church is going to be like.

1. **A Glorious Church.** Paul tells us that the Church will be incredibly glorious or radiant like a bride who has prepared herself for her wedding day (Ephesians 5:25–27). God is going to make the Church holy, so that it is blameless, without stain or wrinkle or any other blemish.

2. **A United Church**. Jesus prayed that the Church, made up of His disciples, would be totally united in heart and purpose (John 17:20–23). He does not want there to be any divisions, but that we would come to the 'unity of the Spirit' and the 'unity of the faith' (Ephesians 4:3, 13).

3. **A Victorious Church**. Jesus said that His church would be so victorious that even the very gates of hell would not be able to stop it as it advances (Matthew 16:18).

What a project! It sounds like something worth living for. However, it doesn't take too much discernment or spiritual insight to see that we aren't there yet. Often, the Church of today isn't too glorious, united or victorious. But don't lose heart, it's starting to happen! God is at work.

The Glory of the Last Day Church

After Jesus finished His work of redemption through His death and resurrection, He returned to heaven. From there, He poured out the Holy Spirit on one hundred and twenty praying disciples. On the day of Pentecost, the Church was born! With limited natural resources and no modern day technology, these Spirit-empowered disciples passionately obeyed the Great Commission (Matthew 28:18–20). The gospel spread rapidly and with great power. Thousands of people were added to the Church of Jesus Christ. The early Church impacted their world!

Despite such an awesome start, things began to decline within a few generations. Through persecution and the infiltration of false doctrine, many Christians compromised and some deserted the faith. The Church became institutionalized and lost much of its early zeal and sense of purpose.

But God is into restoration. He has promised that the glory of the last day Church will be greater than the first Church (Haggai 2:9). He is saving the best for last and we are privileged to be living in those times. One thing we know for sure – Jesus will not return until all the things that have been spoken by the prophets are fulfilled (Acts 3:19–21). When God starts something, He definitely finishes it!

Let's Get to Work!

So what does all this mean for us? Well, it's time for us to roll up our sleeves and become diligent co-laborers with Jesus Christ (1 Corinthians 3:9). If He is still building His Church, then we need to focus the best of our time, energy and resources on helping Him.

You are called to be a part of God's purpose on earth right now (Romans 8:28; 2 Timothy 1:9). You weren't saved just to go to heaven. You are a chosen generation (2 Peter 1:9). You have a calling and a destiny in God. Catch a vision of God's purpose for your life and for the Church of Jesus Christ. Let it motivate you to live a life of purpose and destiny (Proverbs 29:18).

Together, we can see the Church transformed and fulfill its God-given destiny. The world is waiting. Let's get to work to help the Church change.

Notes

1. For a thorough explanation of the biblical teaching on the Church, I recommend the book *The Church in the New Testament* by Kevin J. Conner (Melbourne, Australia: KJC Publications, 1982)

Understanding Church Growth

Church Growth

I have been privileged to be an active part of two growing churches, **City Bible Church** (formerly known as Bible Temple) in Portland, Oregon, USA and **Waverley Christian Fellowship** in Melbourne, Australia. Being part of a growing church is an exciting and joyful experience.

When it comes to the subject of church growth, there seem to be two extreme attitudes today:

1. **Ambition.** This causes an extreme focus on *fruitfulness* and *quantity*, which can lead to competitiveness.

2. **Apathy.** This causes an extreme focus on *faithfulness* and *quality*, which can lead to complacency.

I believe that God wants us to have a healthy desire to maximize our God-given potential. We must have a passion for both faithfulness (quality) **and** fruitfulness (quantity).

God wants the Church to be healthy and to grow. He wants to bring increase. God is interested in numbers. The Bible has a whole book on it! Each number is a person whose life matters to God. The early Church, as recorded in the book of Acts, had people being **added** to it every day (Acts 2:47). That's a minimum of 365 converts every year! Eventually, there was such a **multiplication** of disciples that they lost count of the numbers of people (Acts 4:4; 9:31; 16:5).

Which Model?

But what makes a church grow? Why does one church grow while another does not?

Many people, especially church leaders, are looking for methods that will make the church grow. Everyone is looking for 'the key' to success and church growth. So we look at growing churches and copy what they are doing (methods) while often missing some of the underlying values that are causing the growth (principles).

Today we see many different models or styles of churches:

1. **The Contemporary Model.** Churches that make use of contemporary music and ample use of modern technology are springing up everywhere.

2. **The Seeker-Sensitive Model.** Churches that use a variety of means of communication (e.g. drama) and who endeavor to create a non-threatening environment for unchurched people to hear the message of the gospel.[1]

3. **The Renewal Model.** Churches that focus on prayer and the ministry of the Holy Spirit, often with accompanying physical manifestations.[2]

4. **The Revivalist Model.** Churches that focus on a strong message of repentance through a very confrontational style and approach to ministry.[3]

5. **The Cell Model.** Churches that focus on the formation of a large network of small groups where people gather for fellowship, teaching and outreach.[4]

6. **The Traditional Model.** Churches that continue with the use of established liturgy and traditions in honor of their historical roots.

The amazing thing is that even though there are churches using these models and growing, there are also churches using these models that are not growing. So we can only conclude that the model or the method itself will not automatically cause a church to grow. I say this not to be cynical or critical of any churches using the above models, as we can glean from all of them. The point is that simply copying something that is working somewhere else will not guarantee that your church will grow too.

How does the Church Grow?

In his book, *Natural Church Development*,[5] Christian Schwarz says that rather than seeking to imitate one particular model of church, we should seek to study many churches to discover the universal principles that are relevant for all churches. A **model** is a concept with which some church in a part of the world has had a positive experience. A **principle** is something that applies to every church everywhere. Beneath the surface of every working model, there are principles that can benefit every church.

We can draw some excellent principles from the following scriptures:

> *'See the lilies of the field, **how they grow**.'*
> (Matthew 6:28)

> *'This is what the kingdom of God is like. A man scatters seed on the ground. Night and day, whether he sleeps or gets up, the seed sprouts and grows, though he does not know how. **All by itself** the soil produces grain – first the stalk, then the head, then the full kernel in the head. As soon as the grain is ripe, he puts the sickle to it, because the harvest has come.'*
> (Mark 4:26–29)

> *'I planted the seed, Apollos watered it, but **God made it grow**.'*
> (1 Corinthians 3:6)

We are encouraged to learn, observe, study and research how things in nature grow. We must look not only on the surface, at the **fruit**, but also beneath the surface, to the **roots**. When we look into nature, we see that God causes living things to grow automatically, or all by themselves. There are things we can and cannot do. We can plough the ground, sow the seed, water the seed and harvest the fruit. However, we cannot bring forth the fruit or make things grow. God alone does that through the inherent power within the seed.

So we see that the Church is not some machine that can be programmed, but rather it is a living organism that is designed to grow all by itself if placed in the right environment. No theories can adequately describe the growth of a church. We must seek to understand God's growth principles and release them to work.

This analogy of natural church development teaches us a number of important points:

1. God has designed the church to grow **all by itself.** If He has birthed your church, then He wants it to grow and He has put within its spiritual DNA all that is necessary for it to grow healthy and strong.

2. We must focus our attention on the things that will enhance the growth of the church and remove anything that will inhibit the growth of the church. Just like a gardener, we must be faithful to water, weed and fertilize our ministries and also see that they get enough sun. We must also remove the weeds and bugs that can destroy them.

3. You can't make the church grow, so you might as well sleep at night and not get so stressed. It's growing even when you're asleep!

4. Not every church will be the same size, just as not every seed grows to look the same. True success is maximizing your God-given potential and that of your church or ministry, not being bigger or better than someone else.

5. Not every church will last or live forever. It's an interesting thought to realize that every church we read about in the New Testament no longer exists. Like a plant or even an organization, each church has its own life cycle. However, if we keep it healthy and strong, it can last long enough to reach its full potential.

Rick Warren says, 'The key issue for churches in the twenty-first century will be church **health**, not church growth.' He goes on to say, 'The problem with many churches is that they begin with the wrong question. They ask, "What will **make** our church grow?" The question we need to ask instead is, "What is **keeping** our church from growing?"'[6] God wants His Church to grow. If your church is genuinely healthy, then it will grow!

In the following chapters we will be looking at some important principles that will help the church grow and be healthy. First, we have to come to grips with the fact that things in the church aren't the way they should be. Things have got to change.

Notes

1. Churches such as **Willow Creek Community Church** and **Saddleback Community Church** are examples of churches that are successfully using events designed for those seeking to know more about Christ.

2. The **Toronto Christian Fellowship** is an example of a church that has had a major focus on the renewal of the Holy Spirit, with thousands of people from around the world visiting their meetings and conferences.

3. The **Brownsville Assemblies of God** in Pensacola, Florida is an example of a church that is making a big impact though a strong confrontational message of repentance.

4. There are many strong cell churches around the world including **Yoido Full Gospel Church** in Korea, **Faith Community Baptist Church** in Singapore and the **Bethany World Prayer Center** in Baton Rouge, USA.

5. This book has some good material explaining the key growth factors to the natural development of the church (Carol Stream, IL: ChurchSmart Resources, 1996).

6. These quotes are from Rick Warren's book *The Purpose Driven Church* (Grand Rapids, Michigan: Zondervan Publishing House, 1995), 15–17.

Things Have Got to Change!

The State of the Church

George Barna, in his most thought-provoking book yet, *The Second Coming of the Church*, paints a graphic portrait of the Church in our times. His conclusion is that the next four to five years will determine whether the Church will experience a major revival or whether it will fade into insignificance.

One thing we know for sure is that things have got to change if we are to see the Church be what God intends it to be in the world. Let's not fool ourselves, there's a lot of work to be done and the Church has a long way to go, but remember, the Church is God's project. All we need to do is find out what He wants us to do and how He wants us to do it. When we do that, we are guaranteed success. God always blesses His own projects!

God is in the Change Business

'Change' is a word that many people don't like, because it makes them feel uncomfortable. It always implies leaving the old familiar ways behind and stepping out into new, uncharted waters. It definitely doesn't sound safe. But God is in the change business and His plan requires us to change. We aren't what God wants us to be yet. God is not finished with us. We must move on. We need to change and grow.

The Process of Change

Some change is instant, such as people becoming Christians. In a moment of time, we are born again. Through repentance and faith in Jesus Christ, our sins are washed away. We are cleansed through the blood of Jesus Christ and God immediately sees us as righteous. We are filled with the Holy Spirit, we become children of God and we receive God's nature. Our spirits become alive and we can communicate with our heavenly Father through prayer and worship. Our names are written down in the book of life. God accepts us. This event is called **justification** (Romans 3:22–26; 5:1–2; 8:29–30).

But that's not the end of the story. God then begins a **process** of change in our lives. The soul or inner life needs some work. The mind needs some new thinking patterns programmed into it. The will needs to be surrendered to God and His ways of doing things. The emotions may need some healing and some disciplining. Old habits and ways of living need to be broken and new godly habits need to be established. We need to become what we already are through faith in Christ. This process is called **sanctification** (1 Corinthians 1:2; Ephesians 4:22–23; 1 Thessalonians 4:3).

One day, when the Lord returns, the change will be complete. All sin, sickness, suffering and sorrow will be gone. Our bodies will be changed. This event is called **glorification** (Romans 8:22–23, 30). The beginning is great and the end is too. In between, we are in a time of transition and we must hang on for the ride of our lives.

This process of change can be likened to the incredible transformation of a caterpillar into a butterfly (Romans 12:1–2). Change happens only through the metamorphosis that takes place inside the cocoon. It takes time and it involves a lot of struggle.

So it is with the Church. At times, things might not look too great, but we know that God is in the process of transforming the Church into something beautiful and magnificent. It will take time and there will be some struggle. In the process, the Church must learn to deal effectively with change.

Future Shock

We live in days of unprecedented change. Things in our world are changing so rapidly that many people are suffering from 'future shock'. A popular business consultant recently said this:

'Winds of change are barreling in from all directions.
Competition is tougher than ever and coming from
places you least expected. The customer is more sophis-
ticated and demanding. Technological changes are
incessant. Government regulations are tougher. And
everyone is restructuring, reorganizing, reinventing,
downsizing, outsourcing – all at an ultra sonic pace.
    Don't look for a safe place to wait out the storm,
because these winds are unrelenting. If anything,
they're getting stronger and coming faster, blowing the
shutters off corporate headquarters and small businesses
alike . . . The weather report? More of the same!
    The speed of change is increasing and future changes
will be bigger and come faster, because the rate of
change grows exponentially, not incrementally. So get
ready for the storm of your life. The hurricane season
has just begun.'[1]

That's a good description of the business environment
today, but it also describes the incredible changes that are
taking place in the world around us and therefore we must be
prepared to change also.

We must learn to not only cope with change, but take
advantage of it in order to forge ahead in God's purposes for
our lives. When change is God-ordained, we must not resist
it. We must be ready for it and excited about it.

Although God never changes, He requires us to change
continually. His focus is on the internal and the eternal. The
Christian life is a life of growth and growth means constant
change. God is transforming us by His Spirit into the likeness
of Jesus Christ. He is building us together as a powerful
Church to impact our world. He does this gradually, little
by little, from one level of glory to another (2 Corinthians
3:18).

The Church and Change

Let's face it, the Church doesn't have a good track record
when it comes to change. Churches tend to resist change.
Even if they do accept it, change usually happens with a lot

of pain. We haven't yet mastered how to work our way through change.

You may have heard of the story about the young pastor who decided to move the organ from one side of the platform to the other during his first week in his new pastorate. The Board of Deacons instantly fired him! A few years later this young pastor came through the same town and decided to visit his old church. To his surprise, the organ was on the other side of the platform, the same place he had put it and had subsequently been fired. He immediately went up to the new pastor and said, 'Hey, I got fired for moving the organ over there. How did you do it?' The resident pastor calmly replied, 'One inch per week.'

Someone once said that the last words of the Church will be, 'We never did it this way before.'

Letting go of the old and taking hold of the new is about as comfortable as a trapeze artist must feel when he or she is about to let go of the bar.

Change Readiness

People hold the key to change, and the ability and willingness of individuals to change is the key factor to the future of any group. Change is a process that is both exciting and difficult, and resistance to it is natural and should be expected. The key is to turn resistance into 'change-readiness'.[2]

Change-Readiness is an attitude that is . . .

- open and receptive to new ideas
- excited rather than anxious about change
- challenged, not threatened, by transitions
- committed to change as an ongoing process

Change-Readiness is taking actions to . . .

- anticipate and initiate change
- challenge the status quo
- create, instead of react to, change
- lead, rather than follow

Individuals and churches that are **good** react quickly to change. Individuals and churches that are **great** create change.

We must be forward-thinking people. The apostle Paul made it his aim to forget the things that were behind and to stretch himself forward to what was ahead. He refused to become comfortable or complacent. From his point of view, this way of thinking is a mark of spiritual maturity (Philippians 3:10–15).

In case you didn't notice, God is a God of **new** things. He has made us **new** creations, given us **new** hearts, a **new** spirit, a **new** covenant. We live in a **new** day; we have a **new** name; we have a **new** commandment; we've been given **new** garments; His mercies are **new** every morning; we drink of the **new** wine; we're headed for a **new** Jerusalem and eventually a **new** heavens and earth. In the end, God makes all things **new**!

Embracing the new things God has for us implies leaving the old behind. It requires change and transition. God wants freshness in our lives not stagnation, staleness or sameness. God sent the manna to Israel fresh daily. It couldn't be kept for the next day or it would rot and stink (Exodus 16:12–31). In the same way, we need to keep receiving the new things God has for us. He wants us to be willing, open and ready to change.

Let's Change Gears

My first car had a manual gearshift. It was a little scary, learning to change those gears. Coordinating the movement of my hand on the gear shift and my foot on the clutch while trying to keep an eye on the road took a bit of practice. Sometimes finding that next gear was, 'Grind 'em till you find 'em!'

You can do a lot of damage if you don't learn to transition smoothly between the gears on a car. So it is in leading change in the church. It takes some skill, some experience and lot of good oil of the Holy Spirit.

Knowing when to change is as important as the change itself. If you change too quickly or at the wrong time, things get worse. On the other hand, if you don't change soon enough, you may end up doing some damage and wasting a lot of fuel.

When you reach a certain speed in a specific gear, it is important to make the transition to a higher gear. If you do, you will go faster, yet with less energy. I believe that is where the Church is right now. It is time to shift gears. We must move to a higher level in God so that we can accomplish more with less energy. It is time for us to make some **Strategic Shifts**.

What is a 'Strategic Shift'?

In Old Testament times, there was a group of men from the tribe of Issachar who had *'understanding of the times ... to know what Israel ought to do'* (1 Chronicles 12:32). In contrast, Jesus criticized the Pharisees for being able to read the natural weather patterns, but unable to recognize the *'signs of the times'* (Matthew 16:1–3). The times are changing more rapidly today than at any other point of human history.

God wants us to be a prophetic people who are in tune with His purposes, so that we can be used by Him to accomplish His will in our generation. We must be aware of what is happening in our world. We also need to be aware of what the Spirit is doing and the strategic changes or shifts that God wants us to make.

> A **Strategic Shift** is a 'change of thinking inspired by the Holy Spirit, resulting in a change of behavior that produces a greater effectiveness in fulfilling the purposes of God for this moment in history.'

Seven Strategic Shifts

In the following chapters, we will be looking at seven **Strategic Shifts** that God wants the Church to make:

- **Shift 1** – A *Power Shift* – from self to God.
- **Shift 2** – A *Priority Shift* – from inreach to outreach.

- **Shift 3** – A *Program Shift* – from events to relationship.
- **Shift 4** – A *Leadership Shift* – from ministers to equippers.
- **Shift 5** – A *Ministry Shift* – from consumers to contributors.
- **Shift 6** – A *Worldview Shift* – from a church mentality to a Kingdom mentality.
- **Shift 7** – A *Generation Shift* – from the older to the younger.

Let's now spend some time exploring these **Strategic Shifts** more fully.

Notes

1. This quote is taken from Chapter 1 of the book *Sacred Cows Make the Best Hamburgers* written by Robert Kriegel and David Brandt (Sydney, Australia: HarperCollins Publishers, 1996).

2. These thoughts about change-readiness are also from Chapter 1 of the book *Sacred Cows Make the Best Hamburgers* written by Robert Kriegel and David Brandt (Sydney, Australia: HarperCollins Publishers, 1996).

SHIFT 1

A Power Shift
from self to God

'Power belongs to God.'
(Psalm 62:11, NKJV)

Becoming a Praying Community

A Power Shift

The first shift we need to make in order to help the church change is a **Power Shift**. It is a shift from confidence in self to a greater dependence on God. It is a recognition that true success is, *'not by might or power, but by the Spirit of the Lord'* (Zechariah 4:6). Prayer really is the key to everything both in our personal lives and in the Church.

Pride Goes Before a Fall

One of my greatest learning experiences as a teenager was through an embarrassing failure. My school was involved in a competition with some other nearby schools in areas such as sport and music. Having learned piano for a number of years, I decided to enter the piano solo competition for our school. We also found out that we could enter two people into each category, so I encouraged my younger friend, Todd, to enter, so we could take first and second place. Needless to say, I was overconfident.

The competition began and students from other schools proceeded first. Most were fairly average from my point of view. When it was my turn, I commenced performing a fairly complex piece of music, which I had memorized. I was only into the first few bars of my solo when my mind went completely blank! I meandered on the keys and eventually sat down totally humiliated.

My friend, Todd, then got up and performed his solo. That night, at the awards ceremony, Todd received the first place prize and I failed to qualify.

Travelling home on the bus was a time to reflect and learn from this terrible experience. God taught me that pride really

does go before a fall and that the moment I forget that I am totally dependent on Him, I am in great danger. Like Jesus' disciples, I had to learn that without Him I can do nothing. This important lesson has helped motivate me to remain dependent on God through regular prayer.

I Can Do It!

More recently, as a father, I saw this in an experience with my son, Josiah. Josiah was only about five years old at the time and he was working on a puzzle that was quite difficult for his age. I came over to him and said, 'Can I help you?' Josiah quickly put out his elbow and said to me quite abruptly, 'I can do it.' Well, of course, I didn't want to force him, so I walked away and left him to it.

Within a short period of time, when Josiah had reached a certain level of frustration, I felt a little tug on my jeans. A little voice sheepishly said, 'Daddy, could you please help me?' Like any father would, I said, 'Of course!' So we sat down and finished the puzzle together.

I wonder how many times we continue to struggle because we have said, 'I can do it', while our heavenly Father watches, ready to intervene if we'd only ask for His help.

We see this illustrated in the Old Testament. When King Asa relied on the Lord, victory was guaranteed and thirty-five years of peace followed. When he relied on his own strength and alliances with other kings, he knew what it was to have constant war (2 Chronicles 14:11–13; 15:2; 16:7–9).

Prayer is moving from independence to interdependence. Paul said, '*I can do all things **through Christ** who strengthens me*' (Philippians 4:13). What an incredible balance! That's **confidence** and **humility** in perfect harmony.

Why Pray?

When we don't pray, we are saying to God that we can cope with life by ourselves. We often pray when we are desperate, yet if we would pray and include God in all aspects of our life, we would experience so much more of His blessing and provision.

Jesus lived His life in total dependence and reliance on the Father. He did nothing on His own. He spoke and did what He received from His Father. How? Through prayer!

Jesus said,

> *'I tell you the truth, the Son can do nothing by Himself; He can do only what He sees His Father doing, because whatever the Father does, the Son also does.'*
> (John 5:19; 8:28; 12:49–50; 14:24)

The things that you don't pray about, you believe that you can do by yourself. The things that you do pray about, you believe that you need God's help with. It's as simple as that.

Get Connected

The truth is that we can do nothing of lasting value or eternal worth without God's help. It is only as we are connected to God through prayer that we can be fruitful in our lives (John 15:1–8).

You have probably seen a dry branch that has been broken off the trunk of a tree many weeks earlier. Because it is no longer connected to its life source, it has died and is bearing no fruit. It provides a vivid picture of what happens to our lives without regular connection to Jesus Christ through prayer.

On the other hand, when we are connected to Jesus Christ continually through regular prayer, we position ourselves to receive His life and energy. Like the branch connected to the tree, we are alive and able to bring forth fruit.

What is Prayer?

Prayer, in its most basic form, is simply talking with God. It is a two-way form of communication where we make our thoughts and feelings known to God and He in turn shares with us. It may involve praise, worship, giving thanks, presenting requests, praying for others, listening, meditating or just waiting in stillness.

Prayer is taking time to be with God in intimate conversation. It is based on relationship. Human relationships are dependent on continual communication. In the same way, our relationship with God is built, maintained and developed through regular communication by prayer. It takes time to get to know Him and hear His thoughts.

Prayer can be Powerful

It is not only possible to **know** God through prayer, we can actually **partner** with God in holding back the work of the enemy and in releasing the blessing of God into specific situations.

James tells us that *'the fervent prayer of a righteous person is powerful and effective'* (James 5:16). The prophet Elijah prayed and it stopped raining for three years. He then prayed again and it began to rain. That's powerful prayer! Yet the Bible tells us that Elijah was a man with human frailty just like us. Prayer can really change things.

Every time we pray, God hears and answers. There is a reward for those who pray. Jesus said,

> *'When you pray, go into your room, close the door and pray to your Father, who is unseen. Then your Father, who sees what is done in secret, will **reward** you.'* (Matthew 6:6)

Principles of Effective Prayer[1]

There are many important principles of prayer, including praying with faith (Mark 11:23–24), praying according to God's will (1 John 5:14–15), praying with a pure heart (James 4:2–3) and praying with the power of the Holy Spirit (Romans 8:26).

Let's look at some other important keys to making your prayers more effective.

Desire

Desire is the foundation of a life of prayer. How thirsty are you? Thirst motivates you to come and drink. How desperately do you want to know God? Your desire to know or meet with God motivates you to pray.

The word 'desire' means to crave, to long for, to ask earnestly for, to have a strong affection or yearning for, to reach or stretch out for, to seek, to wish and to have a zeal for. It is an inward impulse or motivation. The Hebrew word literally means to bend, or to turn aside to. It is an inclination. When you are hungry and you are driving along the road, your hunger causes you to 'bend' or to 'turn' off the road towards something that will satisfy that hunger (usually our kids see the 'golden arches' and start yelling 'McDonalds!'). On the other hand, when you are satisfied, you have no hunger or thirst. You are full and have no desire for more.

Desire motivates and directs us. It causes us to seek after something. It motivates us to make decisions directed toward the fulfillment of our desire. Desire precedes and therefore influences all of our choices.

I believe that the Holy Spirit wants to give us a desire or burden to know God more through spending time with Him. We need God, but first of all we need a hunger and a thirst for Him. God responds to desire (Psalm 37:4; 42:1–2; 63:1; 84:2; 143:6; Isaiah 55:1–2; Matthew 5:6; John 4:13–15; 7:37–38; Hebrews 11:6; Revelation 21:6; 22:17). When we ask, we will receive. When we seek, we will find. When we knock, it will be opened to us (Matthew 7:7–8).

Where there is no desire, there is no powerful prayer and no results. Where there is fervent desire, prayer flows naturally and has great power.

Think about **what** you desire. This will reveal your life's direction and purpose. It also exposes the motivation for the choices that you make. Think about **why** you desire it. This will reveal your value system, which reflects your philosophy of life.

We often have desires towards things that don't really satisfy. Our desires can be deceptive. We go after whatever we think will give us what we want. Yet there remains this inner emptiness which is longing to be satisfied. We will either seek satisfaction in humble dependence on God or in proud dependence upon our own resources. Desire and thirst represent an awareness of lack. We often settle for temporary satisfaction but turning to anything other than God will lead to disappointment (Jeremiah 2:13).

Satan will do anything he can to distract us from prayer because he realizes its power! Samuel Chadwick said,

> 'The one concern of the devil is to keep Christians from praying. He fears nothing from prayerless studies, prayerless work and prayerless religion. He laughs at our toil, mocks at our wisdom but trembles when we pray.'

The great prayer warrior, E.M. Bounds, had much to say about the importance of desire and prayer:

> 'Desire is an absolute essential of prayer. Desire precedes prayer, accompanies it, is followed by it. Prayer is the verbal expression of desire. The deeper the desire, the stronger the prayer. Without desire, prayer is a meaningless mumble of words. Such formal praying, with no heart, no feeling, no real desire accompanying it, is to be shunned like a plague. Its exercise is a waste of precious time, and from it, no real blessing accrues.
>
> Pray for desire! Lack of spiritual desire should grieve us, and lead us to lament its absence, to seek earnestly for its bestowal, so that praying becomes an expression of the soul's sincere desire.
>
> A sense of need creates earnest desire. The stronger the sense of need, the greater should be the desire and the more earnest the praying.'[2]

Faith

Another key to powerful, effective prayer is faith. Faith is essential to pleasing God (Hebrews 11:6; Matthew 21:22). Our unbelief causes us to doubt God's existence and His desire and ability to meet us in our time of need. The sin that so easily hinders us is unbelief (Hebrews 12:1).

The Bible tells us that God is willing to hear and answer our prayers. He is not too busy. He is very interested in our lives. He cares about His children because He is our heavenly Father.[3]

In Luke 18:1–8, Jesus tells a story of a persistent widow who finally got what she wanted from a mean judge. It is easy to wrongly interpret this story. We can think of ourselves as the poor helpless widow and God as the judge, who is not really interested in our situation because He is too busy running the universe. Jesus is not trying to tell us to beg and bother God until He finally has to give us what we want just to stop us annoying Him.

No, this story really explains how God feels about our prayers. It is a parable using a study of opposites. We are not like the widow. We have a relationship with the judge, because we are His children and He loves to hear our voice. Secondly, our loving heavenly Father is nothing like this judge. God is righteous, holy and tender, responsive and sympathetic. He wants to bless us (Leviticus 26:3–12; Deuteronomy 28:1–13) and is willing and ready to share His resources with His people. He is a generous and loving Father (Matthew 7:9–11). You are never a bother. He is never too busy and He is not mean.

Not only is God **willing** to help us, He is also **able** to help us. God has all power in the world and He can change any circumstance or any situation. He is able to do immeasurably more than all that we ask or imagine (Ephesians 3:20–21). Sometimes the reason why our prayers are weak is that our faith is weak. We may acknowledge the fact that God is omnipotent but we don't really pray in a way that expects Him to use His power on our behalf. If we did, we would pray more!

In his book, *Too Busy Not to Pray*, Bill Hybels says,

> 'A prayer warrior is a person who is convinced that God is omnipotent, that He has the power to do anything, to change anyone and to intervene in any circumstance. A person who truly believes this refuses to doubt God.'

God wants to be our friend. He is our Father and He longs for us to spend time with Him. He desires to be actively involved in our lives on a daily basis, but He waits patiently for us to include Him in what we are doing.

Sometimes, we may feel that our prayers have not been answered. The truth is that God always hears **and** answers our prayers. However, the answer may not be just what we expect at the time.

Bill Hybels explains it this way:

'If the request is wrong, God says "No".
If the timing is wrong, God says "Slow".
If you are wrong, God says "Grow".
But if the request is right, the timing is right
and you are right, God says, "Go".'

Some requests receive an answer of 'No' because they may be inappropriate, selfish or immature. God does not always give us the things that we want or do things just the way we want them to be done. He often has a higher plan or a more perfect way (Isaiah 55:8–9).

When the timing is wrong, God says 'Slow'. Unfortunately, waiting is not one of our strengths. We live in an instant, fast-paced society where we want everything yesterday. However, we must remember that God's delays are not necessarily denials. We must trust Him and allow Him to strengthen our faith and our character.

Sometimes God wants us to 'Grow', so He doesn't immediately give us the thing we have requested. There may be some areas He wants to change in our lives – new attitudes to be developed, bad habits to change, or relationships to be healed.

When everything is right, God says, 'Go'. Nothing motivates us to pray more than answered prayers!

Let's look at what E.M. Bounds has to say about the importance of faith and prayer.

- Only God can move mountains, but faith and prayer move God.

- Faith gives birth to prayer.

- Lack of faith lies at the root of all poor praying, feeble praying, little praying and unanswered praying.

- Doubt and fear are the twin foes of faith.

- We need men of great faith and men who are great in prayer. These are the two cardinal virtues, which make men great in the eyes of God, the two things which create conditions of real spiritual success in the life and work of the Church.

- We need to be constantly reminded that faith is the one inseparable condition of successful praying.

God does hear our prayers!

'For the eyes of the Lord are on the righteous and His ears are attentive to their prayer, but the face of the Lord is against those who do evil.'   (1 Peter 3:12)

Persistence

Persistence in prayer is essential. Persistence is the ability to hold on, press on, wait and continue until the answer comes. The kind of prayer that influences God is fervent and persistent. Persistence wins where half-hearted indifference fails. In spiritual matters, perseverance succeeds just as in the natural.

The Bible gives us many examples of persistent prayer:

- Abraham interceded for Sodom (Genesis 18:17–33).
- Jacob wrestled all night with the angel.
- Moses prayed forty days and nights for God's anger to be withheld (Deuteronomy 9:18–29; 10:10).
- Elijah repeated his prayer seven times before the rain cloud appeared (James 5:13–18; 1 Kings 18:41–46).
- Daniel, though faint and weak, prayed for three weeks before the answer came (see Daniel 9, 10).
- Jesus spent many nights in prayer. In Gethsemane He presented the same urgent petition three times, yet with an attitude of submission. His victories were all won through urgent persistent prayer.
- The widow persisted with her request until the judge gave her what she wanted (Luke 18:1–8).
- Paul earnestly sought the Lord three times about his *'thorn in the flesh'* (2 Corinthians 12:7–9). He only stopped praying about it when God answered him specifically.

When teaching on prayer, Jesus said, *'Always pray and don't give up or lose heart'* (Luke 18:1). Jesus tells us to 'ask, seek and knock' in prayer. The thought is present continuous – ask and keep on asking, seek and keep on seeking, knock and keep on knocking (Matthew 7:7–8).

When your answers are delayed, don't give up. Continue praying with persistence.

Consistency

Prayer was a daily habit for the believers of the early Church (Acts 2:42).

When we lack consistency, it is much harder to break through in prayer. I like to think of it as the difference between starting a cold motor engine and a warm one. If the engine is cold, you need to prime the fuel pump and pull the choke out. It takes more effort and concentration. In contrast, an engine that is already warm starts immediately. In the same way, it's much easier to pray on a daily basis, even if it is for a short time, than to pray infrequently. Habits form the bulk of our lives. It's what you do regularly and consistently that makes a big difference in your life.

Listening [4]

Close relationships are built on communication, which involves both speaking and listening. In the same way, developing a close relationship with God through prayer involves talking to God and listening to Him. The prophet Amos tells us that there would come a famine of hearing the word of the Lord (Amos 8:11–12). This does not mean that God is not speaking, but that people are not taking the time to hear His voice. God is speaking all the time, but often we are not tuned in to what He is saying.

God communicates to us in many ways through the Holy Spirit. God speaks to us through the Bible, which is His Word. The Scriptures contain God's will for your life and tell us what God is like.

God can also speak to us in our prayer time as we meditate and tune in to the voice of the Holy Spirit within us. The Holy Spirit knows the thoughts of God and wants to reveal them to us (see 1 Corinthians 2:9–16).

There are things that can hinder us from hearing from God such as disobedience (Psalm 66:18), not obeying the last thing God spoke to us (Mark 4:24), distractions, quenching the Holy Spirit (1 Thessalonians 5:19) and closed ears (Jeremiah 6:10; Matthew 13:14–15).

Paul prayed for the Ephesians that they would have a *'spirit of wisdom and revelation'* in the knowledge of God and that the *'eyes of their understanding may be opened to know the hope of their calling, the riches of His inheritance and His great power'* (Ephesians 1:17–18). Paul's one desire was to know God (Philippians 3:10). He wanted to be a close and intimate friend of God, not just a casual acquaintance and He wanted each believer to know God in this same way.

God wants us to be a **prophetic people** who know His heart and mind, then communicate it to the world. Jesus spoke and did only what He received from His Father. In the same way, we are called to be 'ministers of the Spirit', who speak and do what we receive from the Father by the Spirit.

We need to learn to be still and to wait on God. Find a quiet place. Learn to **hear** the voice of God. Learn to **see** the things of God. Ask God to reveal His heart to you – His thoughts and desires. Develop an intimate relationship with God. He is our Father and those who are led by the Spirit are the sons of God (Romans 8:14).

God wants us to abide in His presence. To abide means to remain and to dwell on a constant basis. Prayer can be more than just an event. It can be a lifestyle of living with an awareness of God's presence on a daily basis. Christ lives in you and you can live in Him.

Abraham was called a 'friend' of God because he spent time getting to know God. Abraham was so close to God that God would not act without letting Abraham know first. What an intimate friendship!

Paul Cain once made a statement that has challenged me to this day. He said, 'You can be as close to God as you want to be.' Wow! God has no favorites. He invites everyone to come into His presence and spend time sharing with Him.

A Call to Prayer

Right now there is a global focus on prayer. Christians all around the world are feeling an urgency to pray and intercede as never before. Subjects such as prayer, spiritual warfare, intercession and fasting are becoming highly profiled. There is a call to prayer.

Why is there a such an urgent call to prayer? Frank Damazio, in his book, *Seasons of Revival*, gives us five important reasons:

1. We are in a battle against the spiritual forces of darkness, and prayer is our most powerful weapon (Ephesians 6:18; 1 Peter 4:7; 1 Timothy 4:1).

2. We are living in days of extreme pressure and stress, but prayer will provide us with the resources that we need (2 Timothy 3:1).

3. The problems of mankind are becoming increasingly complex, but through prayer we have access to God's solutions (2 Timothy 3:1–5; James 1:5).

4. There will be times when our faith is severely tested, but prayer will supply the strength that we need to stand (1 Peter 1:6–7; 5:8–10).

5. Our mandate is to take the gospel to our communities, cities and the nations of the earth. Prayer will prepare the way for effective evangelism and mission (Matthew 24:14; Isaiah 2:2).

A House of Prayer

The book of Acts tells us that, in a relatively short period of time, the Gospel went from an upper room (with a few Jews) to all of Asia Minor (a wide variety of Gentiles). The Church spread rapidly throughout Jerusalem, Judea, Samaria and then to the ends of the earth, despite severe persecution.

How did they do it? They had no buildings or modern technology. They simply devoted themselves to the apostles' teaching, fellowship, breaking bread and prayer in homes throughout the city (Acts 2:42–47). Notice that prayer was the only activity mentioned that reached outward. Prayer was clearly the key to their evangelistic success.[5]

The Church was birthed in a prayer meeting in the upper room (Acts 1:14). Pentecost was the answer to their obedient waiting on God (Luke 24:49). Three thousand people were saved on the first day.

The early Church continued to hold regular prayer gatherings, as well as assembling for fellowship, teaching and other purposes (Acts 2:42). The early disciples had tremendous courage and boldness. Wonders and miraculous signs were done and people were added daily to the church. One day, Peter and John were on the way to the temple to pray and a crippled person was healed (Acts 3:1). The church grew to about five thousand men, not including women and children.

A prayer meeting, where God literally shook the building, was characterized by people *'lifting their voices in prayer to God'* (Acts 4:23–31). Their prayer was passionate, intense, fervent and bold. This resulted in great power and grace, with no needy persons among them. The sick and demonized were all healed.

When a crisis developed, the twelve apostles would not allow themselves to be tied down in administrative affairs that would cause them to neglect prayer and the ministry of the Word (Acts 6:1–7). This resulted in the rapid growth of the Church as God's Word spread.

A man by the name of Cornelius prayed to God regularly and God heard him. God directed the apostle Peter, who was up on a roof praying, to go and preach to him (Acts 10:1–48).

Another time, when Peter was in prison, the whole church was praying earnestly for him all night (Acts 12:5,12). God sent an angel to set him free.

The church at Antioch was characterized by fasting and praying. It was in this kind of atmosphere that the first missionary endeavor was birthed (Acts 13:1–3).

Prayer, both individually and corporately, was the key to their success. It was the same for Jesus, the apostles, Paul and the other churches mentioned in the New Testament. Why should it be any different for us today?

What's wrong with us today? Why does the Church have so little impact? Has the promise of Matthew 28:18 failed? Or did the early Church know something we don't? Ed Silvoso says it so well:

'Acts is a book of **prayer** and **power** (both individually and corporately). **Prayer** on the part of men and **power** on the part of God. It was God's power in response to believing prayer (Acts 1:8).'[6]

Paul was the greatest church planter of his time. When writing to his associate Timothy, he said,

> *'I urge, then, **first of all**, that **requests, prayers, interces-sion** and thanksgiving be made for **everyone** – for kings and **all** those in authority, that we may live peaceful and quiet lives in all godliness and holiness. This is good, and pleases God our Savior, who wants **all** men to be saved and to come to a knowledge of the truth. For there is one God and one mediator between God and men, the man Christ Jesus, who gave himself as a ransom for **all** men – the testimony given in its proper time. I want men **everywhere** [all over the city] to lift up holy hands in **prayer**, without anger or disputing.'* (1 Timothy 2:1–8)

Paul wanted Timothy to make sure that the church was a house, or place, of prayer.

The early Church was birthed, sustained and enlarged through prayer. So today, the Church will not be built by our effort alone. In Psalm 127:1, David tells us that unless the Lord builds the house, all our labor is in vain. God's purposes will be accomplished only by God's power working through dependent people, not by human wisdom, strength or innovation alone.

The Church is to be a *'house of prayer for all nations'* (Mark 11:15–17). Prayer must be a priority. Active prayer will turn around churches that aren't growing and help churches that are to advance further. A prayerless church is a powerless church. A prayerful church is a powerful church. It's as simple as that.

Intercession

Prayer is talking with God. Intercession is talking to God on behalf of someone else. All intercession is prayer, but not all prayer is intercession. Intercession literally means 'going between' or 'standing in the gap'. It is pleading with God in order to obtain help for someone in need.

Jesus is described as an intercessor (Romans 8:34; Hebrews 7:25). The Holy Spirit also intercedes for us (Romans 8:27). All intercession is made to the Father.

Some Christians may have a special prayer ministry that enables them to pray for longer periods of time on a regular basis and see frequent answers to their prayers. However, intercession is a role expected of all Christians (1 Timothy 2:1). We are all called to pray for others on a regular basis (James 5:16).

Peter Wagner says, 'The most under-utilized source of spiritual power in our churches today is the exercise of intercessory prayer.'

Pray for Your Leaders

Paul continually asked for prayer from other believers (1 Thessalonians 5:25; Romans 15:30; 2 Corinthians 1:11; Philippians 1:19; Philemon 22). Every Christian needs intercession but especially those in positions of leadership.

Why do leaders need our prayers? Peter Wagner in his book, *Prayer Shield*,[7] lists these reasons:

1. Christian leaders have more responsibility and accountability before God.

2. Christian leaders are more subject to temptation. They are the target of attacks from the world (greed, pride, power, money), the flesh (sex, gluttony, alcohol) and the devil himself (occult and witchcraft).

3. Christian leaders are more targeted by spiritual warfare. The breakdown of Christian leaders' marriages is a primary focus of Satanists. It is sad to see the number of leaders who leave the ministry through burnout, sexual immorality and other causes.

4. Christian leaders have more influence on others. If a leader falls, more people are hurt and set back in their spiritual lives than if others fall. Also, the pastor is one of the major factors in determining the growth or non-growth of a local church.

5. Christian leaders have higher visibility. They are constantly subject to gossip and criticism.

Although prayer for church leaders can never be a substitute for the leader's own prayer life, it can make a huge difference in their life and ministry. Prayer can cause greater effectiveness in the use of their spiritual gifts, a higher level of response to their ministry, more wisdom from God, increased wholeness in Christ, improved attitudes, more evidence of the fruit of the Spirit, better personal prayer lives and improved leadership skills.

Through intercession, there is a partnership in ministry. When you pray for leaders, you participate with them in ministry and along with them receive the blessing of the fruits of their ministry. Daily prayer is more effective than weekly or monthly prayer. Persistent prayer is very important.

Biblical Illustrations of a Power Shift

Joshua and Moses provide us with an excellent example of a **Power Shift**. Exodus 17:8–13 tells the story of Joshua and the Israelites fighting against the Amalekites down in a valley. Moses is up on the mountain lifting his hands in prayer for Joshua and the Israelite army.

As Moses lifted his hands up in intercessory prayer for Joshua and Israel, they began to win the battle. However, when his hands became tired and weary, they began to lose. Prayer made the difference between defeat and victory.

In his book, *Prayer Partners*,[8] John Maxwell gleans some important lessons from this story that give us more significant reasons to pray for our leaders:

1. Godly leaders come under attack (Exodus 17:8). Joshua was at the front of the battle and most vulnerable to attack. Satan watches for the right time to attack Christian leaders. He usually attacks after victory or when the leader is very tired. The devil tempted Jesus during a time of fasting (Luke 4:1–14) and then left him until 'an opportune time'. Satan seeks to attack leaders physically, morally and mentally.

2. Godly leaders can't win the battle alone (Exodus 17:9). No matter how hard Joshua tried, the battle would not be won through his strength and ability.

3. Godly leaders need prayer support (Exodus 17:11). Joshua needed the prayer support of others. When Moses' hands were raised, Joshua and the Israelites were successful.

4. One prayer partner is often not enough (Exodus 17:12). Moses wanted to keep his arms stretched toward heaven in prayer, but even he grew weary and tired.

5. Multiple prayer partners bring the victory (Exodus 17:12–13). Aaron and Hur saw the need, seized the moment and shared the victory. They did everything they could to keep Moses' hands in the air. As a result, Joshua and Israel won the battle.

Today, we need leaders like Joshua, who will lead the battle, and we also need intercessors like Moses, Aaron and Hur, releasing God's power to bring about victory. Prayer makes the difference between defeat and victory. Jack Hayford says,

> 'You and I can help decide which of these two things – blessing or cursing – happens on earth. We will determine whether God's goodness is released toward specific situations or whether the power of sin and Satan is permitted to prevail.'[9]

Prayer and Fasting for Revival [10]

It is time to increase the level and intensity of prayer in the Church. All revivals begin with a call to repentance, which includes consecrating ourselves in prayer and fasting. Only God, through prayer, can help us stand against the attack of Satan upon our nation and enable us to see a spiritual breakthrough.

The Bible records many revivals that began with a consecration of the leadership and the people through prayer and fasting. Jehoshophat, Ezra, Nehemiah, Esther, David, Jehoiakim, Daniel, Joel, Jesus, the Antioch church and the apostle Paul all spent time in intensive prayer and fasting.

This resulted in revival, personal empowerment for ministry, a revelation of God's purposes or a supernatural change of circumstances.

John Wesley said, 'God does nothing, except in answer to believing prayer.' Pray for the entry of God's kingdom and God's will into our world. Prayer makes a difference in our world. Prayer really changes things!

Putting it to Work

It is easy to become so incredibly busy working for God that we neglect taking time to simply be with Him and hear His voice. Like Martha, we become troubled and stressed about **many things** and forget the **one thing** that is most needed, time in prayer (Luke 10:38–42).

We must recognize that our human efforts alone will not be enough to see the Church fulfill its destiny. On the other hand, prayer alone will not be enough. However, bold action accompanied by fervent prayer will see mighty things done for God.

Prayer is the engine room of the Church. Let's make a **Power Shift** by becoming a people of passionate prayer. This shift is vital in helping your church to be transformed.

Notes

1. There are many excellent books on various aspects of prayer. Here are some that I highly recommend: *Too Busy Not to Pray* by Bill Hybels, *Awaken the Dawn* by Ernest Gentile, *Praying with Power* by Peter Wagner, *Intercessory Prayer* by Dutch Sheets, *Possessing the Gates of the Enemy* by Cindy Jacobs and *Seasons of Intercession* by Frank Damazio.

2. From *The Complete Works of E.M. Bounds on Prayer* (Grand Rapids, Michigan: Baker Book House, 1993, pp.29–34).

3. The following section has been adapted from Bill Hybels' book, *Too Busy Not to Pray* (Downers Grove, IL: Inter-Varsity Press, 1988). This book is an excellent practical guide for developing your personal prayer life.

4. There are some excellent books available on learning to hear the voice of God such as *Surprised by the Voice of God* by Jack Deere (Zondervan Publishing House, 1996).

5. This thought is further expounded in Chapter 3 of Ed Silvoso's book, *That None Should Perish* (Regal Books, 1994).

6. From his book, *That None Should Perish* (Regal Books, 1994).

7. This book, *Prayer Shield*, is essential reading for every church leader or anyone who is serious about upholding their church leaders in prayer (Ventura, CAL: Regal Books, 1992).

8. John Maxwell's book, *Partners in Prayer*, is an excellent resource for developing a supportive group of prayer partners for your church or ministry (Thomas Nelson Publishers, 1996).

9. This is from Jack Hayford's classic book on prayer, *Prayer is Invading the Impossible* (Plainfield, NJ: Logos International, 1977).

10. There are a number of good books available on the subject of fasting including *Fasting for Spiritual Breakthrough* by Elmer Towns and *Fasting can Change Your Life* edited by Jerry Falwell and Elmer Towns.

Personal Action Plan

Here are some ideas to help you make a personal **Power Shift**:

1. Develop a daily habit of prayer. Start with a short time of prayer and then gradually increase it.
2. Thank God daily for all the good things in your life. Spend time worshipping and expressing your love to Him. Use some praise or worship music to assist you.
3. Make a list of prayer requests and bring them regularly before God. Spend time praying for yourself, for those you know, for opportunities to witness, for wisdom in decision-making, for help in times of difficulty and for anything that you are worried about.
4. Take time to listen to God speaking to you. Use a journal or notebook and write down things that He tells you.
5. Get with other Christians and pray together.
6. Be faithful to attend any church prayer meetings.
7. Offer to be a prayer partner for your pastor or one of the key leaders in your church. Ask them for specific things that you can pray for.
8. Read some good books on the subject of prayer to help improve your prayer life.
9. Ask someone who is experienced in prayer to mentor you in your prayer life.

Church Action Plan

Here are some ideas for to help your church make a **Power Shift**:

1. Hold regular church prayer meetings. There are so many things to pray about. Pray for the church's needs, the local community, your city, your nation and God's work in other nations of the world.
2. Teach on practical principles of effective prayer.
3. Gather the men or women together for prayer in the church building or in homes.
4. Have a weekly day of prayer and fasting.
5. Establish intercessory prayer groups.
6. Set up a prayer chain for urgent requests or needs.
7. Have a 'prayer requests' card available for people to complete and hand in.
8. Organize or join in with city-wide prayer initiatives.
9. Have a 'prayer walk' through your community.
10. Have a forty-day period of prayer and fasting for the entire church focused on specific requests. Create a roster so that people can choose which days they will fast and pray.
11. Have intercessors praying during the church meetings.
12. Profile answers to prayer through regular testimonies.
13. Form a 'prayer partners' group for the pastor and other key church leaders.

SHIFT 2

A Priority Shift
from inreach to outreach

'... there will be more rejoicing in heaven over one sinner who repents than over ninety-nine righteous persons who do not need to repent.'

(Luke 15:7)

Becoming an Evangelistic Community

Heaven's Priority

Heaven must be a place of continual joy and celebration. However, we know that there is one thing that causes the joy level in heaven to increase exponentially. What is it? When one person becomes a child of God through faith in Jesus Christ! Jesus tells us that there is 'more joy' in heaven over one lost sinner who repents than over ninety-nine others who are still serving God (Luke 15:7, 10). Heaven gets more excited about lost people being found than about any other thing.

Jesus came into the world for a number of reasons, but the primary reason was to save sinners (Matthew 9:13). As Bill Hybels says, 'Lost people matter to God. Therefore, they should matter to us.'[1] Saving lost people is God's bottom line. That's the only thing that brought Jesus out of heaven to earth.

God's heart is for the world. He doesn't want anyone to perish, but all to come to repentance. He wants all people to be saved and to come to the knowledge of the truth (1 Timothy 2:1–4; 2 Peter 3:9). God loved the world so much that He gave His only Son, Jesus, so that anyone who believes in Him might have eternal life (John 3:16).

God has done His part. Jesus has done His part. He went to the cross and took our sin, our judgement and our death upon Himself. He died, the just for the unjust, that He might bring us to God. The Holy Spirit has done His part. He has come to empower, enlighten and encourage us to do our part. What is our part? Our part is to be witnesses for Jesus, reaching out to every person. The Great Commission is our mandate (Matthew 28:18–20; Acts 1:8).

Activities such as prayer, worship, ministry and fellowship are very important. But reaching out to see people saved must become just as important. We need to make a **Priority Shift**, where our focus moves from inreach to outreach.

The Purpose of the Church

The church exists for three primary reasons:

1. **To minister to God.** This has to do with our relationship with God, which we develop through prayer, worship and reading His Word.

2. **To minister to one another.** This has to do with our relationship with other Christians, which is expressed through love, fellowship and serving.

3. **To minister to the world.** This has to do with our relationship with those who do not yet know Jesus Christ as Lord and Savior, and is expressed through evangelism, community outreach, church planting and missions.

The interesting thing about these three important ministries is that the only one that can't be done in heaven is number three. In fact, if we are only here for the first two reasons, then we might as well go to heaven right now! In heaven, it will be so much easier to love God, because we'll see Him face to face. It will be easier to love one another in heaven, because we'll all be perfect. The only reason we're still here on earth is that God is longsuffering, not wanting anyone to perish, but all people to have an opportunity to receive eternal life.

In heaven, there will be no more evangelism. While we're on earth, we should mix with the unsaved and cultivate friendships with them. Our life goal should be to go to heaven and take as many people with us as possible.

Reach Out!

The ministry focus of the Church must change from inreach to outreach. The Church exists for mission, not just for itself. Churches that focus on maintaining their tradition alone, without seeking to reach out to embrace the lost, will eventually become irrelevant and possibly extinct.

The Church must avoid becoming **isolated** from the world.[2] Unfortunately, most Christians have very few friendships with non-Christians and even less as time goes on. We may work with them, but we don't spend time with them socially. We can be so radically different that we find it hard to relate to their world and culture. We have a message, but no audience. We become irrelevant.

The other extreme is to be so **immersed** in the world and become so like them that there is no noticeable difference between the Church and the world. We have an audience, but our message has no impact.

Worse still is when we **compromise** by becoming a citizen of both worlds and at home in both of them. We are neither radical nor different, and therefore we are no longer salt or light.

The challenge is to identify with the world and reach out to people in love without compromising. Like Paul, we are to become all things to all men to save some. We are called to be **in** the world, but not **of** the world. God wants us to be both different and relevant.

The Church must infiltrate the world for Christ. It must have a harvest focus by passionately pursuing the Great Commission (not the Great Omission). Churches that remain healthy and continue to grow will put tremendous energy into reaching the unchurched, into missions and into church planting.

God wants more than faithfulness to Him. He wants fruitfulness. He expects a harvest. As Rick Warren says, He wants us to 'catch fish not just look after the aquarium'.[3]

God wants to put His heart of love in His people once again. A love that reaches out to all kinds of people and embraces them, regardless of their condition. He wants the Church to be inclusive, rather than exclusive, in its attitude. Our mission is to reach out in love and express compassion for the needs of people. We are to share the good news that Christ can reconcile them to God. We are to make disciples of all nations. It's time for the Church to reach out as never before.

Church Growth

God wants the Church to grow! He wants us to be fruitful (Genesis 1:22; Matthew 21:19). God longs to see multitudes saved all over the world (Acts 1:8). The Church is never too big when there are still more people to be saved. If the entire city has been saved, only then are churches in it big enough!

Church growth analysts tell us that the Church can grow in three different ways:

1. **Biological growth.** Biological church growth comes from new babies being born to families already in a local church. Praise the Lord for children. They are a blessing from the Lord. It is important to raise our children in the ways of the Lord so that when they are old they continue to love and serve God.

2. **Transfer growth.** Transfer church growth comes from people who move to a church after they have already become Christians through another church or ministry. In a highly mobile society, it is common to see people moving from place to place and this often involves finding a new church. People move churches for a variety of other reasons also. These include a hunger for more teaching, better programs for children and youth, doctrinal reasons, unresolved conflicts or leadership failure. Transfer growth does happen but it is not 'kingdom growth'. It is simply a reshuffling of the saints who are already saved.

3. **Conversion growth.** Conversion church growth comes from people who become Christians as a direct result of the ministry of a local church. In the early church, The Lord added to the church daily those who were being saved (Acts 2:47). Wouldn't it be great if every church won at least one convert for every day of the year. That's 365 new Christians per year per church!

Unfortunately, statistics indicate that approximately eighty percent of churches have plateaued and fifteen percent are growing primarily by attracting Christians from other churches. Only five percent are effective in winning unchurched people consistently.

Do the Work of an Evangelist

If you have an evangelistic gifting, then reaching people for Christ is second nature for you. But if you're similar to me, then you'll find it a challenge. I've grown up in the church and my major gifts are preaching and leadership. I have never seen myself as an evangelist and I haven't grown up under strongly evangelistic ministries.

Not long after taking the role of Senior Minister of our church, I realized the need to strengthen the evangelistic ministry of our church. We had grown rapidly, but mainly through transfer growth.

A change had to take place in my heart. My priority had to become evangelism and God spoke to me very clearly that I was to *'do the work of an evangelist'* (2 Timothy 4:5). What is the work of an evangelist? It is to equip people to share their faith confidently, to stir up a passion for lost people and to ensure that the church has a strong focus on evangelism. I had to begin making a **Priority Shift**.

Four Spheres of Outreach

As we shift our priority to reaching people for Christ, there are four different areas or spheres of outreach to focus on.[4]

1. Inside the church

Many people will visit your church meetings, from time to time, for one reason or another. How you treat these people will have a big impact on whether or not they return and on their acceptance of Jesus Christ.

The singing may be great, the preaching inspiring and the building comfortable and clean, but if no one speaks to visitors, they are unlikely to return. God has a special love for the 'strangers', or the people who are new or unknown. He wants us to reach out to them and include them.

Many people will come to Christ through coming and seeing what God is doing amongst His people. That is why church outreach events can be a very important tool in the process of reaching people for Christ. After all, a living vibrant church is an excellent testimony for Jesus Christ.

2. Your friends

Each Christian already has a network of friends and contacts with people who do not yet know Christ. You are placed strategically to reach certain people others may never reach.

The Great Commission tells us to **go** into the world. Many people will never **come** to a church meeting. The church gathers for meetings, but still remains the church as it scatters throughout the city during the week. Each Christian needs to be wise in the relationships they have with people outside the church, and ready for opportunities to witness for Christ (Colossians 4:2–6). People make the best witnesses!

How can the church average at least one convert per day? Only personal soul winning will accomplish the task. We cannot just have church meetings. Soul winning is a ministry for the whole church. Don't limit it to the specialists – evangelists and preachers. We can all win people to Jesus!

There has been a wide variety of methods and strategies used over the years to win people to Christ. Here are some of the common ones:

- Evangelistic crusades with bold gospel preaching.
- Special events such as concerts or musical programs.
- Personal witnessing.
- Street witnessing and door knocking.
- The media, including television, radio and literature.
- Small groups and special interest groups.
- Seeker services.

Although many of these methods have been and continue to be effective, nine out of ten people come to Christ as a direct result of relationships.

3. Your community

There are many people in our local community who do not go to church and who do not have a friendship with a Christian. We must go to them. What a huge mission field we have right on our doorstep. Unsaved people are not commanded to go to church. Jesus told His disciples,

'Go out into the highways [roads] *and hedges* [country lanes] *and compel them to come in, that my house may be filled.'*   (Luke 14:23).

We are surrounded by opportunities to extend Christ's love. People in need are often very open and receptive to the gospel. We must get out into our communities and begin to reach out. Jesus went about simply doing good and helping people at their point of need (Acts 10:38). He was then able to move on to talk about the important spiritual issues of life (John 4:1–42).

Practical ministries of compassion, such as feeding the poor, providing clothing and shelter, as well as offering counseling, can form a wonderful bridge between the church and the people in our local community. Each church has a responsibility to make a difference, right in their immediate locality.

4. The world

The final sphere of outreach is the entire world, made up of people who will never visit your church, who you don't know personally and who are not nearby. God calls us to have a heart for these people who are far away.

The Great Commission is to go into **all** the world, to preach the gospel to **every** person and to make disciples of **all** nations, or ethnic groups.

This can be done through church planting and missionary enterprise. Every church must have a heart for the world. Join forces with other churches and ministries. Reach out both far and wide to those who have never heard.

You Can Be a Soul-Winner!

God wants every Christian to be a soul winner. Jesus told the disciples, *'I will make you fishers of men'* (Mark 1:17). You may be timid, like Timothy, but you can *'do the work of an evangelist'* (2 Timothy 4:5). God wants to give you the power and boldness to witness for Him (Acts 1:8).

We can all be involved in the ministry of soul winning. It may be through prayer, financial support of evangelistic ministry, inviting someone to a church meeting or leading someone to Christ personally.

Although some Christians have a specific gift or ministry of evangelism, all of us are called to be witnesses for Jesus Christ. We don't even need to pray about it. Just do it!

Here are some keys to successful soul-winning.[5]

Faith

It takes faith to win people to Christ. Firstly, we need to have faith in the gospel itself. We must believe that Jesus really is the answer to people's problems. No doctor is going to be excited about prescribing a medicine he or she does not believe in. In the same way, we will not be motivated to share about Jesus unless we have confidence in Him.

Next, we need to have faith that people are looking for God and an answer to their problem. Believe that people really are basically hungry to know God and to be saved.

Finally, we need to have faith in the fact that God can use us. Until we believe it in our mind, we will never do it. If we say we are not evangelistic, then we probably never will be. Our thoughts about ourselves can limit us. We must see ourselves as God does.

It's not always easy to be a witness. We won't always be accepted (Matthew 5:11–12). The enemy will try to immobilize and silence us through guilt, condemnation or fear. He wants to hinder the message of Jesus from being shared, because he knows it can set people free.

God can use us just the way we are. We have been chosen and uniquely equipped to reach a certain group of people that no one else may reach. Let faith arise in our hearts and motivate us to step out and be soul-winners for Jesus.

Compassion

We must love people before we can win them. Jesus would often go out amongst the crowds of people, see their need and then be moved with compassion to help them (Matthew 9:35–36). Like Jesus, we must get out of our comfort zones and the safe routines of our life. We need to be moved by compassion to touch needy people where they are. Compassion is an attitude towards people that expresses itself in love, kindness and genuine interest.

If we have a lack of concern or love for the lost, we will not be motivated to witness to them. Even methods and strategies are useless unless we have a passion for people who don't know Christ. We need God's heart of love in our lives.

Within the first few years of becoming a Christian, we tend to cut off our friendships with non-Christians or lose the motivation to witness to them. How easily we become consumed by our own world of problems and challenges, so that we miss opportunities to help others who may be in greater need.

We must be motivated by love for people, not by guilt, fear, manipulation or a sense of obligation. Evangelism must be a passionate priority for the Church, because it is nearest to the heart of God. Passion has to the foundation for evangelism. Paul said, *'The love of Christ constrains* [or compels] *me'* (2 Corinthians 5:14).

Jesus was a *'friend of sinners'* (Matthew 11:19). He took time to be with them. He treated people as valuable and important. Often people don't care how much you know until they know how much you care.

Jesus told the story of the good Samaritan to show us that we must love our neighbor. Our neighbor is anyone in need (Luke 10:25–37). When we are moved by the needs, problems and hurts of people around us, we become motivated to point them to the answer, Jesus Christ.

Courage

Many times we want to share our faith, but we are scared. Fear immobilizes us because the things we fear, we tend to avoid. The things we don't fear, we do easily.

What are some of the fears we might experience during witnessing? Here are a few for starters:

- Not knowing what to say or becoming tongue-tied
- Having to answer difficult questions

- Fear of the unknown
- Rejection
- Alienating the person
- Being challenged or put in an awkward position
- People may get upset with us

Numerous questions and thoughts fill our mind. 'Is it really worth it?' 'Maybe it's too great of a risk.' 'Why not leave it to the experts or the "green beret" evangelists?'

Let's face it, fear is normal. Even the great apostles were fearful at times (Acts 4:29–31). Fear is something that we have to continually deal with. In fact, you may never witness if you're waiting for the fear to go and some special feeling to come. Don't allow fear to control you and stop you from being obedient to the command we have been given to witness for Christ.

God tells us not to fear. There are about 1500 verses on the subject of fear in the Bible. There are approximately 365 times where God says, 'Fear not!' There's one for every day of the year!

Fear is a battle of the mind. I know that I would never be where I am today if I had not faced my fears head on and moved forward in faith. One thing we know is that fear does not come from God (2 Timothy 1:7). Fear tries to stop us at every point of our journey with God. Courage is not the absence of fear, but the conquering of fear.

Believe that God wants to use you. Have a love for Jesus that is greater than your fear of witnessing. A positive emotion can overcome a negative one. Usually, both are active during witnessing. Be filled with the Holy Spirit. He has come to help you overcome your fear and give you the power to be a bold witness for Christ.

Step across the line. Get out of the boat. Get out on a limb. That's where the fruit is. Move out into the deep. Be bold. Stretch. Don't become satisfied or comfortable.

You can turn from being a wimp into a warrior, and from a person bound by fear into a person motivated by faith. If you think you can or you think you can't, you'll be right both times. What will it be? Fear or courage?

Preparation

The apostle Peter tells us,

> *'But in your hearts, set apart Christ as Lord. Always be prepared to give an answer to everyone who asks you to give the reason for the hope that you have. But do this with gentleness and respect.'* (1 Peter 3:15)

Preparation in witnessing is very important. What should you be prepared for?

1. For opportunities

Be prepared for opportunities that will come and be willing to seize the moment. Always be ready to speak up.

2. To share our testimony

Your personal testimony can be very impacting. To be a witness, you don't have to be perfect, just forgiven and a friend of Jesus. Share what Jesus has done for you and what He means to you. Your personal experience is real and very powerful (John 4:28–30; 39–42; 9:13–34).

3. To present the gospel

We need to study and prepare ourselves so that we have an answer for the hope that we have within. We must be able to give reasons and evidence for our faith.[6]

Paul was always ready to make a defense of his faith in Jesus Christ and for the message of the gospel (Acts 22:1; 24:10; 25:8; 26:1–2). In the same way, we need to be ready to share the gospel with those with whom we come in contact.

What is the gospel and how is it different from religion? One way of explaining it is that religion is spelt 'DO'.[7] Religion tells us to try to do enough to earn God's favor and to feel good about ourselves. It centers on what I can accomplish through my own efforts. Salvation becomes a reward for my own achievements. The focus is on self-reliance. It says, 'Pile up the good deeds and minimize the bad ones and you'll get to heaven.' The trouble is that all of our efforts fall short of God's standard. The result is spiritual death or separation from God.

Even good works don't save you. Nicodemus was a very religious person who had tried to do what was right all of his life, yet he was told by Jesus, *'You must be born again'* (John 3:3).

In contrast, Christianity is spelt 'DONE'. It centers on what Christ has done for us. He accomplishes what we never could. He paid the price for our sins and offers us forgiveness. When we accept Him, condemnation goes and salvation is ours. Best of all, it's a free gift. However, it's up to each person to respond and receive it through repentance and faith.

4. To lead someone to Christ

There are four basic steps that a person needs to take in order to receive Jesus Christ as their Savior and Lord:

- **Confess** (1 John 1:9–10). They must admit their need.

- **Repent** (Acts 17:30; 3:19–20). They must be willing to change and to live differently.

- **Believe** (John 3:16,36). They need to believe that Jesus is God's Son, who died for their sins and can forgive them.

- **Receive** (John 1:12). They need to receive Jesus into their life through a prayer of invitation. They must ask Him to be their Savior and Lord.

Here is a simple prayer that you can lead the person in:

'Dear heavenly Father, thank You loving me so much that You sent Jesus to die for my sin. I ask You to forgive me for all that I have done wrong. Fill me with Your Holy Spirit. Make me Your child. Make me new. I will live for You. I will serve You all the days of my life. Amen.'

The Bible says that if we confess that Jesus is Lord and believe it in our hearts, we will be saved (Romans 10:8–10).

5. To help them grow

Be willing to follow up and help new Christians. We want conversions and changed lives, not just decisions and prayers prayed.

They will need assurance of their salvation. If we ask Jesus into our life, He **will** come in (Revelation 3:20). This is based on **fact** not **feeling**. If Jesus said it, then it happens.

Help them to grow spiritually[8]. They will need to be shown how to:

- Talk to God in prayer every day.

- Study the Bible in order to know God better (2 Timothy 2:15). God's Word teaches us how to live.

- Worship, fellowship and serve with other Christians. This includes attending church gatherings (Hebrews 10:25).

- Tell others about Jesus. They need to make a public confession (Matthew 10:32–33). We are not to be ashamed of Jesus.

- Obey the commands of Jesus. They need to be water-baptized, filled with the Spirit and begin to love God and others.

We witness and share our faith. The Holy Spirit convicts and draws people to Jesus. The Father births people into His family. We welcome them and help them to grow and make a positive contribution.

Wisdom

Proverbs 11:30 says, *'He that wins souls is wise.'* It takes a lot of wisdom to witness effectively and to lead someone to a commitment to Jesus Christ as the Lord of their life.

We need to understand that evangelism is a process. Most people go through a long pre-conversion stage. It takes time for people to move from a position of resistance to the gospel to a place of readiness to receive. Don't rush the process or force people. It takes wisdom to know where each person is on their spiritual journey and then to encourage them to take the next step. Be patient and don't give up.

As in any harvest, one person ploughs the ground, one plants the seed, one waters it and one reaps the fruit. All rejoice together and receive reward for their work. It is God who makes things grow and gets the glory. We get to be co-workers with Him (see 1 Corinthians 3:5–9). Keep sowing the seed. God will bring the increase.

Each one of us is unique and God has equipped us to reach certain types of people based on our personality, style and background.[9] As we go about our daily interaction with people around us, God will give us opportunities to share the good news of Jesus Christ.

Let's follow Paul's advice:

> *'Be wise in the way you act toward outsiders; make the most of every opportunity. Let your conversation be always full of grace, seasoned with salt, so that you may know how to answer everyone.'* (Colossians 4:5–6)

You can be a soul winner!

Small Group Evangelism

Each one of us can be a witness for Jesus Christ, but we can also join with other Christians in this important ministry. We'll be talking more about Cell Groups in the next chapter, but for now, let's realize that small groups can be very effective in reaching people for Christ if they have an outward focus.

In the Old Testament, the nation of Israel failed to achieve God's plan because they were inward looking and introverted. In the same way, there is always a danger that, as people develop close relationships with other Christians in a small group, they can become isolated from those outside the group. Although there is a place for these sorts of relationships in certain types of support groups, this should be avoided at all costs in a normal Cell Group. A Cell Group must open its doors to friends, neighbors, relatives and other new people. God wants us to look outward, so that we can be a blessing to others.

Does your Cell Group have a 'No Vacancy' sign over it?

- No 'physical room' – the home setting is too small or the group is too large.

- No 'emotional room' – the group is already full of its own emotional needs.

- No 'relationship room' – new people would be seen as a distraction from your wonderful relationships.

- No 'communication room' – more than twelve communication lines are too many.

- No 'leadership room' – leaders are not able to nurture new members.

A Cell Group should be an **outreach group**, where Christians can bring their friends, neighbors and relatives in order for them to experience the life that is in Jesus Christ.

Cell Groups can provide the prayer, support, encouragement and accountability that is required to help people make this important **Priority Shift**. Cell Groups also provide the best means for following up and discipling new converts to Christ. They provide a sturdy 'net' of relationships so that the ingathering of souls is not lost.

Reaching New People

Here are some ways for your group to reach out to new people:

1. Look out for visitors or new people during Sunday church meetings and other church events. Be friendly and invite new people to your Cell Group.

2. Ask each member of your group to think of someone they know who is not in a Cell Group and then invite them along.

3. Pray for unsaved friends and relatives as a group. Keep track of their progress.

4. Have a discussion on the subject of evangelism and how you could reach those who don't know the Lord. Come up with some creative strategies for your Cell Group.

5. Plan informal activities around hobbies or general interests and then host a Cell Group meeting catering for unchurched people. Event evangelism can be through the **front door** of large celebration gatherings or through the **side door** of small Cell Group meetings.

6. Look for people with an evangelistic gift in your group and encourage them to be the initiator of any Cell Group outreach activities.

7. Work together as a group to make good use of church events that are designed for bringing unchurched people along.

8. Cultivate an 'empty chair' atmosphere, where you are always thinking about who will next join your group. Refuse to allow your Cell Group to become introverted.

By doing these things, we can develop an outward and others-centered focus. We also provide opportunities to see others come to the joy of knowing Christ.

Be Fruitful and Multiply!

God wants fruitfulness, not just faithfulness. Jesus said,

> *'This is to my Father's glory, that you bear much fruit, showing yourselves to be my disciples.'*   (John 15:8)

In the early Church, the Lord began by adding new people daily to the church as they met regularly in the temple courts and in their homes. Eventually, the church began to multiply rapidly.

As your Cell Group grows, the need will come for it to be multiplied (not divided!). If you don't eventually multiply your group, then it will either become too large and the dynamics of a Cell Group will be lost, or the group will become ingrown.

Healthy Cell Groups multiply. Your goal, if you are a Cell Group Leader, should be multiplication not maintenance. To prepare for multiplication, you will need to appoint an apprentice leader. Your aim is to fully train your apprentice leader over a period of time. This involves more than just delegating. It requires sharing all aspects of what it takes to lead a Cell Group.

Jesus led the disciples toward taking over His ministry, gradually releasing more and more responsibility as they moved from one stage to the next. In the same way, Paul told Timothy to focus his equipping and training on those who had a vision to pass it on (2 Timothy 2:1–2).

Every Cell Group should have a normal life cycle, which refers to the time it exists before multiplication. If the concept of multiplication is talked about at the start of the group, this can reduce the potential pain of the actual multiplication process. People are prepared for it and accept it as healthy.

The Benefits of Sharing your Faith

Just as the most exciting place in a hospital is the maternity ward, so one of the most exciting places to be in church is around new Christians.

Sharing your faith benefits God by bringing Him glory and great joy. Sharing your faith benefits others by bringing them to salvation, abundant life and into a new family. Sharing your faith benefits you by bringing personal joy, satisfaction, growth and confidence in God. Together, let's make a **Priority Shift** by making heaven's priority ours. Help to transform your church by winning the lost for Christ.

Notes

1. Bill Hybels, Senior Pastor of **Willow Creek Community Church**, has had a tremendous influence on the Church by helping Christians develop a greater passion for reaching the lost for Christ. For some outstanding training on personal evangelism, see the book *Becoming a Contagious Christian* by Bill Hybels and Lee Strobel (Grand Rapids, Michigan: Zondervan Publishing House, 1994). This material comes as a training course with a teacher's guide and videos.

2. For further discussion on these thoughts about isolation, immersion and compromise, see Joe Aldridge's book *Lifestyle Evangelism* (Portland, Oregon: Multnomah Press, 1981).

3. Rick Warren's book, *The Purpose Driven Church*, has some excellent material on evangelism and reaching people for Christ.

4. These four spheres of outreach are explained more fully by Frank Tillapaugh in Chapter 8 of the book *Mastering Outreach and Evangelism* (Portland, Oregon: Multnomah Press, 1990).

5. Many of the following thoughts on soul winning have been gleaned from John Maxwell's tape set *Successful Soul Winning Kit*, available from INJOY (Atlanta, Georgia: 1992).

6. For some excellent material to help you give logical reasons when defending your faith, see Josh McDowell's book *Evidence that Demands a Verdict* (San Bernadino, California: Here's Life Publishers, 1981).

7. This simple, but effective way of comparing Christianity and religion is from the course *Becoming a Contagious Christian* by Bill Hybels and Lee Strobel (Grand Rapids, Michigan: Zondervan Publishing House, 1994).

8. Follow up of new Christians is essential. This may be done personally through one-to-one discipleship or in a group setting in the form of a New Christians' class. An excellent course your church may like to start is the ALPHA course, which helps new Christians establish their faith in Christ and which is also very good for people who are interested in learning more about Christianity.

9. Part Three of Rick Warren's book *The Purpose Driven Church* has some very good material on targeting different types of people for evangelism.

Personal Action Plan

Here are some ideas to help you to make a personal **Priority Shift**:

1. Decide to become a soul winner.
2. List five people you would like to be saved. Pray for them daily and for God to use you to win them. Then contact them every week in some way. Do something special for them once a month. Include them in special activities. Look for opportunities to witness or share your faith. [Statistics reveal that if you will do this, two out of the five will be saved in a year and one more in the second year!]
3. Be a friendly person who always looks out for new people.
4. Intentionally make friends and develop relationships with people who are not Christians.
5. Begin to pray for opportunities to share the love of Jesus.
6. Invite your non-Christian family, friends or relatives to an appropriate church event.
7. Read a book or attend a seminar on personal evangelism. Develop and train yourself in this important ministry.
8. Talk to someone who is experienced and good at personal evangelism and ask them to mentor you.
9. Get involved in following up new Christians in your church. Ask them how they came to Christ and learn from them.
10. Ask God for a vision for the harvest. See it happening.

Church Action Plan

Here are some ideas to help your church make a **Priority Shift**:

1. Form a team of people whose specific aim is to reach out to visitors at your celebration events. Set up a visitor's lounge. Offer visitors a free gift, a visitor's guide or help with any needs they may have.

2. Find out the greatest needs in your local community and then start a ministry to meet these needs. Network with other similar ministries.

3. Host a free Christmas dinner for needy families in the community.

4. Develop a program for children or youth during their school holiday times.

5. Consider developing a qualified counseling team that can provide help and support for special needs within your church and to people in the community.

6. Teach people how to witness effectively and how to lead their friends to Christ. This can be done through sermons or seminars.

7. Host some special events where the gospel is preached with relevance and power. Plan these events with the unchurched in mind. Remember that Jesus is sensitive to seekers.

8. Have new Christians testify about how they came to know Jesus.

9. Make opportunity on a regular basis for people to give their lives to Jesus during your church meetings. Every meeting has needy people attending. Give them an opportunity to respond to Jesus. Help people make a public commitment and confession of their faith.

10. Focus the congregation constantly toward outreach.

11. Develop a world mission ministry within the church. Have a regular emphasis on reaching the world for Christ. Send out short-term teams to other nations, give financial support to mission workers and network with other ministries.

12. Consider planting a church with a team of people from your church. Church planting is one of the best methods of evangelism.

13. Study what other evangelistic churches are doing in order to learn principles that you can apply to your own church.

14. Allocate an above-average amount of money and resources for evangelistic activity.

SHIFT 3

A Program Shift
from events to relationship

'A new command I give you: Love one another.
As I have loved you, so you must love one another.
By this all men will know that you are my disciples,
if you love one another.'
(John 13:34–35)

Becoming a Caring Community

A Program Shift

The next shift that the church must make is a **Program Shift**. This shift requires a change of emphasis from **events** to **relationships**. God wants us to shift our focus from just having events to the development of meaningful relationships between people, so that the church becomes a caring Christian community.

For too long, church has become a thing we go to, an event or an experience, rather than a community of people networked together in loving relationships. The Church is to be much more than a crowd gathering for an event. It is to be a closely networked group of people serving Christ together. Genuine loving relationships provide the care that people need and the context in which life transformation can take place.

Known By Our Love

In John 13:34–35, Jesus said,

> *'A new command I give you: Love one another. As I have loved you, so you must love one another. By this all men will know that you are my disciples, if you love one another.'*

The Church is God's **new community** that is to be known by its love and the quality of relationships between people.

In Acts 2:41–47, we see the distinguishing qualities of this new community. These first believers ate together, prayed together, shared their material possessions, praised God together, met together to learn the Word of God and experienced opportunities to witness about Jesus Christ. As they did, they attracted others from the city to follow Jesus Christ and be a part of their community.

Loving others requires maturity. Have you ever thought about what makes a mature church? Here are some of the most common answers that people give:

1. **An active church.** Some believe that a mature church is a church where there is much activity taking place as people zealously serve and give their time to church events and ministries.

2. **A growing church.** Some believe that the evidence of maturity is church growth. If the numbers are increasing and the church is getting bigger, then it must be mature.

3. **A giving church.** Some believe that financial giving is an indicator of maturity. If everyone is generous in their giving, maturity is evident.

4. **A soul-winning church.** Some believe that dynamic evangelism is evidence of maturity. People being saved regularly is what it's all about.

5. **A missionary-minded church.** Others believe that a mature church is one that is sending people to the nations to preach the gospel.

6. **A smooth-running church.** Others believe that an orderly and well-organized church is evidence of maturity.

7. **A Spirit-filled church.** Still others believe that the key to maturity is the activity of the Holy Spirit. The power of God and the gifts or manifestation of the Holy Spirit mean that the church is mature.

I believe that many or all of these things will be present in a mature church, yet it is possible to have all of them and **still not have** a mature church.

Paul made it clear in his letters to various churches that what thrilled him the most was the evidence of faith, hope and love amongst the believers, and especially love. He was most pleased when he saw that these things were being developed.[1]

- **Faith** is the confidence and trust that a local church has in Jesus Christ.

- **Hope** is the optimism and sense of security that a local church has, especially in regard to their present and future relationship to God through Jesus Christ.

- **Love** refers to the relationships that exist in a local church, as well as the way that local group relates to all people. In essence, love is the manifestation of Christ-like behavior by a group of believers.

Out of these three important qualities, the greatest or most important is love. It is greater than status, power, success or money. Love is the essential nature of God Himself and love is to be the primary concern of each Christian and each local church. In all that we do in church, we must be careful not to neglect this important quality of love.

When Paul wrote to the Ephesians, the Philippians, the Colossians and the Thessalonians, he began his letters by thanking God for the love that was being reflected in each church (Ephesians 1:15; Colossians 1:3–6; 1 Thessalonians 1:2–3; 2 Thessalonians 1:3–4). But when he wrote his first letter to the Corinthians, he made no mention of love in his opening remarks. He only thanked God for the grace being manifested amongst them, for they were a very gifted church. However, they were not mature. They were still baby Christians who had not grown up. They were not a loving community. They were carnal and selfish and therefore he had to rebuke them.

The church at Corinth had many spiritual gifts but they had no love. They were gifted yet immature. That's why Paul wrote the great chapter on love – 1 Corinthians 13. Everything they did reflected carnality, not love. He contrasts their weakness with reflections of what true love is really like.

1. They were impatient with each other and unkind in their attitudes toward each other. There were serious divisions and quarrels taking place in the church. In contrast, true love is patient and kind.

2. They were envious and proud. They were boastful and jealous of each other. Love does not envy. It does not boast and it is not proud.

3. They were putting each other down and using their gifts to glorify themselves. True love is not rude or self-seeking.

4. They were actually taking each other to court before non-Christian judges. No one was wise enough to settle a dispute between believers. In contrast, love is not easily angered and it keeps no record of wrongs.

5. They were wronging and defrauding each other and there was immorality in the church. They were not filled with grief over their own sin. In contrast, love does not delight in evil, but rejoices in the truth.

6. They were insensitive to weaker members and they were not protecting each other thereby causing others to stumble. True love always protects, always trusts, always hopes, and always perseveres.

7. They emphasized spiritual gifts, rather than love, as a sign of maturity. In reality, gifts are temporary and will pass away. Love alone will remain and continue.

When measured against the standards of true Christian love, the Corinthians fell short on every count.

The New Testament gives us a direct command to 'love others' over fifty-five times. God wants our love to grow and mature (Philippians 1:9–11; 1 Thessalonians 4:9–10; 1 Peter 1:21–22). The greatest commandments are about love because life is all about loving God and loving people (Matthew 22:34–40; Romans 13:8–10; Galatians 5:13–14).

Love is more than a feeling, an attraction or a passionate drive. It is a decision to do good to another person and it often involves attitudes and actions that must be expressed in spite of personal feelings. Jesus went to the cross because He loved us, not because he relished the feeling of incredible pain He would have to go through. Love is demonstrated through qualities such as patience, kindness, unselfishness, humility, forgiveness, honesty, unity, peace and righteousness.

The Church is to be a caring community of mutual loving relationships. Our deepest need is to be loved, to be accepted and to be forgiven. People need care more than they need excitement. They need to belong, not just believe. Unfortunately, many churches have 'crowded pews but lonely people'.

God's Church Program

God works His purposes out through two aspects of church life:

1. The large gathering ('temple' or 'celebration').[2]
2. The small gathering ('house' or 'cell').[3]

These two gatherings are like the two wings of a bird that help the Church keep balance and move forward effectively. A church with an overemphasis on only one of these gatherings will tend to go in circles and make little forward progress.[4]

This balance of large and small gatherings is demonstrated throughout the Scriptures:

1. **The nation of Israel.** This church of almost three million people had three annual gatherings for the entire nation called the 'Feasts of Israel' which were festival celebrations. However, the entire nation was divided into twelve tribes, which were further broken down into clans and families. These interacted regularly throughout the year (Numbers 1:2–4). God wanted each individual to belong to a family, even if they were a foreigner (Psalm 68:6). Moses also appointed leaders over various group sizes, from tens all the way up to thousands, in order to help mobilize and care for this huge church (Exodus 18:19–26).

2. **Jesus Christ.** Jesus loved the crowd and He ministered to multitudes of people, sometimes in gatherings of up to five thousand people (Matthew 9:36–38). However, He devoted His prime time to a small group of twelve disciples.

3. **The early Church.** The first Church had huge gatherings of thousands of people in the temple courts. They also met together in small groups in homes throughout the city (Acts 2:42–47; 5:42; 20:20).

We need both large and small gatherings of believers. If we only focus on the large gathering, or major on it to the neglect of the small gathering, we will not achieve God's purposes.

Why Celebration Events?

A celebration event is when an entire local church gathers together. Something special happens when a lot of people gather together with a hunger to meet with God. It is to be a time of celebration characterized by enthusiasm, excitement, inspiration and joy.

There are many reasons to gather together with other Christians in a celebration event.

1. To minister to the Lord through corporate prayer and worship.

2. To receive teaching from God's Word.

3. To outwork our God-given corporate purpose and direction.

4. To fellowship with other believers.

5. To demonstrate our unity as a group of believers.

6. To invite unchurched friends so they can hear the gospel.

There are some important keys to creating dynamic church gatherings: [5]

1. Our attitude should be that we are gathering together unto the Lord first of all. We are not just attending another church meeting. God has called us out of our homes to meet with Him. He has made an appointment with us and He expects us to be there. He promises to be there personally whenever two or three gather together in His name. When God shows up, something good is always going to happen.

2. We should be committed to attend celebration events on a regular basis. Christians who neglect church meetings tend to drift in their faith. Paul tells us not to neglect meeting together regularly, and all the more as the

coming of the Lord gets closer (Hebrews 10:25). We should not turn up to a church meeting just because we have nothing else to do. It needs to be a priority in our life.

3. We should attend church meetings with an attitude of faith and expectancy. This releases God to work in a powerful way. When there is complacency and apathy, even God is limited in what He can do (Mark 6:5–6). Dynamic gatherings require an anointing, not only on those who lead worship and speak, but also on the congregation who contribute and respond with an attitude of faith.

Why Small Groups?

God's purposes cannot be achieved through the celebration event or large gathering alone. Imagine what would happen to your church if it had no building and no public meeting. Most churches would disintegrate because they are built solely on events.[6] In the event of persecution, such as that experienced recently in China, small groups alone would enable the Church to continue to grow and expand.

A good celebration event alone does not make for a healthy, growing church. This is because of the limitations of the celebration event:

1. Close relationships cannot be built in a celebration event.

    On Sunday morning, most churches have people sitting in rows looking at the neck of the person in front. Although we worship and receive teaching together, we can't really get to know other people intimately in this kind of environment. We might say 'Hello' and 'How are you?' before or after the event, but there's usually no time to get beyond the 'Fine, thank you' and 'See you next week' kind of conversations.

    Also, in a large gathering, you can remain somewhat anonymous because you may not be acquainted with the people around you. It can be similar to attending a major sports event. The only way to develop a caring community of believers is to foster relational networks of Christians through small groups.

2. Not every person can receive personal care in a celebration event.

   We may be able to pray for one another during or at the end of the meeting, but the time required to give each person focused care and attention is usually not available in this kind of event.

3. Not every person can contribute or minister in a celebration event.

   In most churches, there usually isn't time for each person to share something with the group. The majority of the people at a church meeting usually sit, sing and listen for the entire time of the meeting without being able to give any personal contribution. Usually, only the few people who lead, minister from the platform, or facilitate the practical aspects of the meeting have an opportunity to grow in the use of their gifts.

4. There is no accountability for what is taught in the celebration event and there is no way to personally disciple, coach or mentor people.

   As wonderful as the church event may be and as inspiring as the message may be, it is possible for people to attend, say 'Amen' and then do absolutely nothing about what they have heard once the meeting is finished. Many churches move on from week to week with new teaching material, assuming that everyone has done what they heard last week. In reality, this is often not the case.

The wonderful thing is that these important things can all be achieved in a small gathering of believers. That is why the small group must be seen as **primary** to the purpose of the church and not as a secondary option or an add-on. The Koreans did not invent small groups! They are part of God's program for the Church. We must shift to a more biblical paradigm of **celebration** (large gathering) and **cell** (small gathering).[7]

The Cell Church

The cell-based church is a growing phenomenon because of its emphasis on small group life as well as the corporate excitement of celebration events. Larry Stockstill says, 'Quality small group ministry prepares the church for harvest and hostility' (or persecution).[8]

Most churches tend to add more and more programs as they grow. Although each program may have a good cause, the end result is a very busy church schedule, competition for resources (volunteers, budget and space on the church calendar) and a lack of alignment of ministries.

The cell-based church doesn't necessarily eliminate all of the programs of the church. However, it provides the possibility of refocusing them through the small group paradigm. Christians networked together in small groups can take on almost all of the ministries of the church in an extremely effective manner.

It is important that we understand why the Church should make this shift to Cell Groups. Here are some important reasons:

1. Cells are biblical.

2. Cells promote true Christian community and quality relationships.

3. Cells are the only way to pastor a growing congregation.

4. Cells are the best way to disciple people.

5. Cells are the best way to raise up new leaders.

6. Cells are the best way to mobilize believers into effective ministry to one another and to the unchurched. Ministry is decentralized and delegated to high performance teams of believers.

7. Cells are the best way to assimilate new people, both visitors and new Christians.

8. Cells prepare the church for the possibility of persecution.

9. Cells bring simplicity to the ministry of the church. Many of the church's programs can be run more effectively through Cell Groups.

10. Cells can reduce the competition between departments for volunteers.

11. Cells build holistic ministry because evangelism, assimilation, care, service, prayer, training and multiplication can all be done through the one ministry program.

12. Cells have helped the world's largest churches keep growing while still maintaining quality care and discipleship.

I believe that each church needs to embrace the strengths of the cell-based church without losing the importance of celebration events and corporate vision.

The Purpose of Cell Groups

I believe there are four primary purposes for Cell Groups in the Church. These can be expressed in the following purpose statement.[9]

1. **A Cell Group is a *care* group.** 'It is a place where Christians can gather together to care for one another through friendship, encouragement and practical expressions of love and kindness.'

2. **A Cell Group is a *disciple-making* group.** 'It is a place where Christians can grow together to become fervent followers of Jesus Christ through the process of discipling, teaching and mentoring.'

3. **A Cell Group is a *ministry* group.** 'It is a place where Christians can develop and use their God-given gifts and abilities to help others.'

4. **A Cell Group is an *outreach* group.** 'It is a place where Christians can bring their friends, neighbors and relatives in order for them to experience the life that is in Jesus Christ.'

We addressed the fourth purpose statement back in Chapter 2 when we talked about making a **Priority Shift**. We will amplify the second and third purposes in the next few chapters. For now, let's look at the first one.

A Cell Group is a *Care* Group

'It is a place where Christians can gather together to care for one another through friendship, encouragement and practical expressions of love and kindness.'

This **Program Shift** requires us to see quality relationships as a priority. People need to be connected to others in loving relationships that provide care, belonging and inspiration for personal growth. Our goal should be to see every person loved and cared for in such a way that they feel accepted, valued and have a sense of belonging. This is done best in a small group.

Church and Christian life must take place in the context of relationships. In fact, most of the New Testament focuses on relationships. Notice the many 'one another's' in Paul's writings to the Church. Most of these things can only realistically take place in a small group of people.

The leader of a Cell Group has the primary responsibility to ensure that his or her small group is a place of love and care. Here are some ways that this can be done:

1. Seek to develop a quality relationship with each person in your group and encourage them to do the same with one another.

2. Express interest in one another's personal and family life through asking questions and active listening. It is really important to take the time to get to know one another. Find out how long they have been a Christian, the level of their spiritual maturity, their family background, their career, their church involvement, their hobbies and personal interests, their friendships, their hopes and dreams as well as their fears and concerns.

3. Encourage them to be warm towards one another through sensitivity and kindness.

4. Encourage them to be aware of what is happening in one another's lives. What issues, challenges, decisions or pressures are they facing right now?

5. Encourage them to help, visit and pray for one another during times of need. Jesus really emphasized the

importance of caring practically for people (Matthew 25:34–46). People respond well to being cared for and this is one of the keys to having a successful Cell Group.

6. Encourage them to meet together informally for a meal or social event outside of the group meeting.

These things will help the Cell Group Leader build a good relationship with each person, which will be a foundation to seeing them grow in Christ. Demonstrating and providing care helps you gain rapport, develop trust and establish credibility as a leader. There is a deep cry in people's hearts to be cared for. It is only when people know that you genuinely care for them that they will allow you to speak into their lives. Good times of fellowship and care make a real impact on people's lives.

Proverbs 27:23 tells us to

'Be sure you know the condition of your flocks, give careful attention to your herds.'

This is a challenging verse for all Senior Pastors, especially of growing churches. A large network of small groups is the only effective way to provide quality care for a lot of people. Primary care happens in the Cell Group, not from the pastor or church staff.

Is Church a Safe Place to Be?

In Ephesians 2:8–10, Paul tells us that we are God's workmanship, which literally means a product or a fabric that God is making. God starts with raw materials and then, through a process, He completes His unique design. We are all 'under construction' and would benefit from a sign on us that says, 'Please be patient, God is not finished with me yet.'

We have been justified by grace through faith. One day we will be glorified, which means that sin will be gone, resulting in us becoming perfect and mature. In between then and now, we are being sanctified, which is a process of putting off the habits of the sinful nature and putting on the habits of God's nature within us.

In every church, people are at various points of spiritual maturity. There are spiritual 'fathers and mothers'. There are strong 'sons and daughters' and there are growing 'children and babies' (1 John 2:13–14).

Each of us needs to realize that often behind our Sunday smiles,[10] many people may be struggling with things such as:

1. Addictions such as drugs, smoking, alcohol or pornography.
2. Sin habits or patterns of compulsive behavior that are hard to break.
3. Traumatic experiences or hurts in the past that may be hard for them to let go of and put behind them.
4. Stresses and persistent problems that are hard to cope with.
5. Pain from sexual abuse or immoral tendencies.
6. Broken relationships, such as separation or divorce.

Many people are broken and hurting. What do these people do and where do they go? Is it okay to not be okay? People like this have only two options:

1. They can fake it and pretend to have it all together. Eventually, they will give up and quit on church and God, because they're tired of playing the game.
2. They can admit that they are struggling and receive acceptance and help in a loving community. This is what the Church is supposed to be.

Grace and Truth

As we develop relationships with other people, we must constantly balance grace and truth. Jesus was full of both (John 1:14).

Truth focuses on the ideal world and on things such as absolutes, law, standards, righteousness, holiness, godliness, character, convictions, ethics and morals. Grace focuses on the real world and on things such as love, forgiveness, acceptance, care, encouragement, compassion and help.

Truth without grace results in harshness, legalism, condemnation and fear. On the other hand, grace without truth results in compromise and hypocrisy.

Are our relationships filled with grace and truth? Do we seek to heal, help and cover our brothers and sisters? Or are we critical, judgmental and condemning in our attitudes toward one another? Is there gossip and prejudice in the Church?

Helping Those Who Are Struggling

When people fall and fail, we must reach out to help them in a spirit of love. Though a righteous person falls or trips up seven times, they will rise again (Proverbs 24:16)!

Paul says, in Galatians 6:1–2,

> *'Brothers, if someone is caught in a sin, you who are spiritual should restore him gently. But watch yourself, or you also may be tempted. Carry each other's burdens, and in this way you will fulfill the law of Christ.'*

When someone has done something wrong, we should confront him or her lovingly. Jesus tells us, in Matthew 18:15–17, that when someone sins, we should go to them alone and sort it out. If this doesn't work out, we must take two or three others along. If they still refuse to hear, we should take it to the entire church. If they still refuse, we are told to excommunicate them from the Christian community and treat them as an unbeliever (1 Corinthians 5:9–13). However, church discipline is always focused toward the hope of restoration.

So we see that if people recognize their problem, want help and are trying to change, then we are to work with them. If they blatantly refuse to change, then their sin requires that we not fellowship with them and pray that they will come to repentance. God wants us to warn and urge one another towards holy living (2 Timothy 4:2; Titus 1:13; 2:15).

Sometimes people struggle with problems and difficulties that are beyond the ability of the average Christian or Cell Group Leader to help. The development of trained and competent people, who are gifted as counselors, can provide important support for the care ministry of the church. Sometimes people need professional support and guidance as they go through the process of change, whether it be breaking a habit, dealing with their past or healing a broken relationship.

The Power of Love

God's love in us can heal and bring change to people's lives. Rules and demands can't do this. God wants the Church to be a place of love and acceptance, forgiveness and grace, encouragement and exhortation so that people have a healthy environment in which they can change.

Jesus' love was grace-filled, warm, caring, friendly, sacrificial, giving and healing. We see this in His approach to the Samaritan woman, who had been divorced five times and was now living with another man (John 4:17–18). She had a bad reputation, but Jesus reached out to her in love to lift her up.

In John 8:3–11, we have the record of the Pharisees bringing to Jesus a woman involved in adultery. After the Pharisees had left feeling ashamed, Jesus said to the woman, *'Neither do I condemn you.'* That was **grace**. He then said, *'Go and sin no more.'* That was **truth**.

God works from the inside out. He works on our hearts or our inner thoughts, attitudes and motives. If our thinking can change, then our behavior will follow. So often, we focus on external behavior, which can result in mere conformity without any true inner change or transformation.

Love in Action

We must focus on doing things that build loving and healthy relationships. The New Testament mentions numerous positive things that we should do to, or for one another. Here's a brief list:[11]

1. *'Love your enemies and pray for those who persecute you'* (Matthew 5:44).

2. *'Love your neighbor as yourself'* (Matthew 22:39).

3. *'Love one another'* (John 13:34).

4. *'Follow the way of love'* (1 Corinthians 14:1).

5. *'Do everything in love'* (1 Corinthians 16:14).

6. *'Serve one another in love'* (Galatians 5:13).

7. *'Be patient, bearing with one another in love'* (Ephesians 4:2).

8. *'Live a life of love, just as Christ loved us and gave himself up for us'* (Ephesians 5:2).

9. *'Speak the truth in love'* (Ephesians 4:15).

10. *'Husbands love your wives, just as Christ loved the Church and gave Himself up for her'* (Ephesians 5:25).

11. *'And over all these virtues, put on love'* (Colossians 3:14).

12. *'Pursue . . . love'* (2 Timothy 2:22).

13. *'Let us consider how we may spur one another on toward love'* (Hebrews 10:24).

14. *'Love the brotherhood of believers'* (1 Peter 2:17).

15. *'Above all, love each other deeply, because love covers over a multitude of sins'* (1 Peter 4:8).

16. *'Let us not love with words or tongue but with actions and in truth'* (1 John 3:18).

We must also avoid things that destroy relationships such as envy, jealousy, insensitivity, strife, anger, conflict, quarrelling, competitiveness, prejudice, judging, selfishness, hatred, pride, gossip, slander, favoritism, rudeness, criticism, possessiveness, unrealistic expectations and lack of forgiveness.

We must get rid of these kinds of things and allow the Holy Spirit to fill us with His love so that we can become people who build up others at every opportunity. We should see each person through God's eyes – as someone who Christ died for and who is very precious and valuable.

Each individual Christian is responsible to make the church a caring community of people, and the health and growth of the church is directly related to the way we treat one another.

1. The body will *'build itself up in love, as each part does its work'* (Ephesians 4:16).

2. The body will build itself up in love when there is *'equal concern for one another'* (1 Corinthians 12:25).

3. The body will build itself up in love when we *'carry each other's burdens'* (Galatians 6:2).

4. The body will build itself up in love when we *'submit to one another out of reverence for Christ'* (Ephesians 5:21).

5. The body will build itself up in love when we *'forgive one another'* (Ephesians 4:32).

6. The body will build itself up in love when we *'encourage one another and build each other up'* (1 Thessalonians 5:11).

7. The body will build itself up in love when we are honest with one another (Colossians 3:9).

8. The body will build itself up in love when we *'offer hospitality to one another without grumbling'* (1 Peter 4:9).

9. The body will build itself up in love when we *'teach and counsel one another with all wisdom'* (Colossians 3:16).

10. The body will build itself up in love when we *'confess our sins to each other and pray'* (James 5:16).

A Friendly Church

As we make this **Program Shift**, our goal is to gather Christians, non-Christians, unchurched and needy people together. Reaching people is our focus – all kinds of people, regardless of their age, social position or ethnic background. To win them, we must attract them. To attract them, we must love them and show interest in their lives by helping to meet their needs. Friendliness accompanied by warmth and genuine care will make a difference.

Jesus gathered and attracted people. People of all ages and backgrounds wanted to be around Him because He cared. Crowds of people followed Him. There was something about Jesus that attracted people. It was His heart, His smile, His honesty, His concern, His simplicity, His acceptance and

His love. Remember, people don't care how much you know until they know how much you care.

Jesus longed to gather all the people of Jerusalem together under His protective care. His arms were outstretched to everyone. No one who came to him was turned away, no matter what race, social status, gender, physical, moral or spiritual condition (John 6:37).

The religious leaders, on the other hand, were consumed with rules and regulations but had no personal relationship with God. They were separate from and above the people. They condemned people, put heavy burdens on them and excluded themselves from people. No wonder people weren't crowding around them!

In the early Church, people were daily being drawn and added to the Church. Jesus was in the midst and through His Church He was attracting and gathering people.

Is your church gathering people? What does it feel like to visit your church community? Here's an example of what people look for when they come to your church.[12]

> We have heard of a man who, in an attempt to find out what other churches were really like, visited 18 different churches on consecutive Sundays. He always sat near the front of each sanctuary. After the service, he would walk slowly to the rear, then return to the front and back to the rear again using a different aisle. He was neatly dressed, smiled pleasantly at other worshippers and he would make it a point to initiate a conversation with at least one other person. He would also remain for coffee if it were served.
>
> He used the following scale to rate his reception:
>
> - 10 points for a smile from a worshipper.
>
> - 10 points for a greeting from a worshipper.
>
> - 100 points if a worshipper exchanged names with him.
>
> - 200 points if he was invited to another service.
>
> - 1000 if he was introduced to another person.
>
> - 2000 points if he was invited to meet the pastor.

On this scale 11 of the 18 churches earned less than 100 points. 5 churches received less than 20 points. His conclusion was this: the doctrine may be biblical, the singing inspirational, the sermon uplifting, but when visitors find that nobody cares if they are there or not, they are unlikely to return.

How does your church rate?

Corporate Culture

Each church develops a personality or a culture of its own. Some people call this **corporate culture**. The culture of a church is a reflection of its leaders and its members. What does it feel like to be a visitor in your church? Think about it. The size of your church has nothing to do with it. I've been in a small church of less than twenty-five people and no one spoke to me. On the other hand, I've been a church meeting with thousands of people and felt very welcome.

To attract and gather people we must love them, accept them, care for them, be friendly to them and be hospitable to them (1 Timothy 3:2; Titus 1:8).

Each one of us must look beyond ourselves whether you're at church, at home, at school or at work. We must seek to understand, relate to, love and care for people. As long as we are pre-occupied with ourselves, we will be ineffective as disciples of Jesus.

The Church is not an event, a crowd or an audience. It is a community of people, joined together through loving relationships, that heal and restore. This kind of church community will bring transformation to people's lives and present an answer to our needy world. Together, let's make a **Program Shift** in order to help transform our church.

Notes

1. These concepts are fully expanded in a book called *The Measure of a Church* by Gene Getz (Glendale, California: Regal Books, 1975).

2. In this book, a 'large gathering' will refer to any group over twenty people, as the dynamics of a small group really change once the number reaches more than twelve people.

3. There is a wide variety of names used for small groups in churches. These include names such as 'Home Fellowship Groups' and 'Care Groups'. In this book we will use the term 'Cell Groups'.

4. This analogy is from a book called *The Second Reformation* by William Beckham (Houston, Texas: Touch Publications, 1995).

5. For further teaching on this subject, see the book *The Dynamics of Corporate Gatherings* by Frank Damazio (Eugene, Oregon: Church Life Library, 1986).

6. William Beckham further elaborates this thought in his book *The Second Reformation*.

7. Carl George's book, *Prepare Your Church for the Future*, further amplifies the concept of Celebration and Cell (Tarrytown, New York: Fleming H. Revel Company, 1991).

8. Larry Stockstill's book, *The Cell Church*, is a good overview of the benefits of a Cell Church and how it functions (Ventura, California: Regal Books, 1998).

9. This statement was adapted from an original *Statement of Purpose* for *Lifecare Groups*, the small group ministry of Bible Temple (in Portland, Oregon), where I attended from 1971–81.

10. This phrase, 'Behind our Sunday Smiles', is borrowed from a book by the same title written by Jimmy Ray Lee (Grand Rapids, Michigan: Baker Book House, 1991).

11. Gene Getz has an excellent series of books that amplify the 'one another's' of the New Testament (*Loving One Another, Building up One Another, Encouraging One Another, Praying for One Another, Serving One Another*, Wheaton, IL: Victor Books, 1981).

12. Source unknown.

Personal Action Plan

Here are some ideas to help you make a personal **Program Shift**:

1. Make an effort to meet someone new, or reach out to someone you don't know very well, each time you attend a church meeting.
2. Get involved in a small group in your church and contribute to it.
3. Invite people to your home for a meal or a time of fellowship. Include people you may not know very well.
4. Read books on the subject of relationships and develop an ability to relate to a wide variety of people.
5. Learn to ask questions. Be a good listener. Take a genuine interest in other people.
6. Make a list of people who are on the fringe of your church. Call them on the telephone or spend some personal time with them. Try to help them connect with other Christians in your church.
7. Develop yourself. Work through any hurts or hang-ups you may have from previous negative experiences. This will give you more confidence in relating to other people.
8. Resolve any offences you have. Make a commitment to keep a clear conscience so that you can go to sleep every night knowing that no one has anything against you that you haven't taken care of.
9. Learn some basic counseling skills. Read a book or attend a seminar. Equip yourself to help other people with their problems and struggles.

Church Action Plan

Here are some ideas to help your church make a **Program Shift**:

1. Start a small group ministry in your church. Train your leaders well. If you have an existing small group ministry that is not going well, revitalize it.

2. Intentionally develop a friendly atmosphere in all your church events. Encourage people to interact and develop relationships.

3. Establish a counseling ministry for people who are hurting and encourage them to seek help.

4. Avoid filling up the weekly schedule with too many church meetings. Make time for people to spend time together socially and to develop relationships.

5. Have church social events designed for people to get to know one another.

6. Train all church leaders in people helping skills. Remember that we are in the people business.

7. Have all ministry leaders write notes of thanks and encouragement to their people regularly.

8. Resolve any offences or conflicts immediately.

9. Have a regular visitation or 'tele-care' program, where you contact everyone in your church in person or over the phone to see how they are.

SHIFT 4

A Leadership Shift from ministers to equippers

*'He gave some ... to equip the saints
to do the work of the ministry.'*
(Ephesians 4:11–12)

Becoming Empowering Leaders

A Leadership Shift

The fourth shift that the church must make is a **Leadership Shift**. This shift requires church leaders to change their focus from doing ministry themselves to raising up more ministers. Even in the business world, there is a shift taking place to servant leadership, empowerment, delegation, high perform-ance teams, creating vision ownership and the value of the individual.

Church leaders need to take on the role of a **coach**, who empowers others to reach their ministry potential. This is leadership the way God designed it – equipping and mobiliz-ing others into effective ministry.

Gathering, motivating, training and mobilizing people must become a major priority in the church. Developing people as effective ministers is vital to the ongoing growth and health of the church and its ministries.

Leadership Style

Carl George, in his book *How to Break Church Growth Barriers*, uses an excellent illustration of the change needed in leader-ship style within the Church today.[1]

> 'Imagine a country hit by a devastating earthquake where 50,000 people are either injured or dead. Two medical teams, each headed by a doctor, are being airlifted to the heart of the disaster area.
>
> John, the doctor leading the first team steps out of the helicopter and is overwhelmed by what he sees. There, right in front of him, workers are pulling a body from the rubble. Moved by compassion, he rushes over and calculates the personnel and equipment needed to help

this victim. He assigns half his team and half his supplies to work on this person.

A handful of survivors notice the doctor and bring him another victim. This person is in a worse condition. The doctor assigns the rest of the team and resources to care for this person. Now what? There are still 49,998 people, but already his resources have been spent on two people.

He decides to make himself more available. He and his staff will push themselves harder. They will be on call 24 hours a day, seven days a week, to treat as many people as possible.

Result? Within a few weeks, this doctor is forced to go home. His body has not kept pace and through lowered resistance, he's caught one of the diseases rampant in the disaster area. Everything comes to a standstill until a replacement arrives.

Bill, the doctor leading the second medical team also is deeply shocked and moved by compassion toward the massive death and pain evident when they arrive. There's widespread malnutrition, open wounds and other horrible conditions. People are suffering and dying before their very eyes.

They quickly decide that, by themselves, they are inadequate for the task. So, instead of attending to the first person in sight, they follow a plan that will reach a maximum number of people in the least amount of time, using their scarce resources.

Let's train some people to help us. One group will make sure safe drinking water is available, another will take care of shelter issues, another with food. Another group will work on waste control and public health, by working on the sewer system before it mixes with the water supply. This will prevent the growth of infection.

They train the healthier survivors to serve as health officers. They focus on remedial and interventionary care, starting with the people who, if treated, have a good chance of recovery. They give priority to those who are getting well, so that additional workers can help reach others.'

Which team was more caring? Actually, both had equally strong feelings of love and compassion. However, they differed in **how** they showed their concern.

John is the typical **shepherd** style of leader. He is the primary caregiver. He is driven by people's expectations and is always available. He does all the ministry himself, which creates dependency. He doesn't delegate and he plans poorly. He also ignores the trends or the big picture. He can only do so much before burning out.

Bill is more of a **rancher** style of leader. He sees the big picture, takes leadership and mobilizes other people. He has a group focus and gives himself to supervision and planning. Through mobilizing others, he provided for a higher level of long-range care and a multiplication strategy that resulted in more people being helped.

Biblical Leadership Models

What is the most biblical style of leadership? Let's look at a few examples:

1. Moses was the great leader of the church in the wilderness. However, he tended to do everything himself when it came to leadership responsibilities. He was the original 'one-man-band'! The problem was that he was wearing himself out and the people weren't getting very good service. It took his kind father-in-law, Jethro, to give him a word of wisdom that enabled him to mobilize others to help him in the work of the ministry (Exodus 18:13–27).

2. Nehemiah was an excellent leader, who led a group of people to rebuild the wall of the City of Jerusalem after it had been destroyed by the Babylonians. The task was too big for him to do by himself, so he made sure every person had a place and a job to do to contribute to the overall task. He fulfilled the mission through mobilizing others to catch the vision and working to accomplish it (Nehemiah 1–6).

3. Jesus was a shepherd, but He worked like a rancher. He trained twelve disciples and told them to go and make

more disciples, who would raise up even more disciples and thereby multiply the ministry (Matthew 28:18–20). Jesus was the perfect coach. He chose His own team and then invested time into helping them understand God's vision for them. He helped each one of them grow and develop. Eventually each took his place in leading the Church.

4. The Apostles of the early Church refused to leave their primary duties of prayer and the Word of God to attend to the urgent demands of a newly emerged problem. Instead, they delegated this responsibility out to a new group of leaders and thereby multiplied the ministry (see Acts 6:1–7).

5. Barnabas demonstrated the qualities of a good equipping leader. He saw the potential in Paul before the Apostles did and he helped establish him in ministry (Acts 9:27–28). He stood with Paul during the good times and the difficult times (Acts 13:2; 13:50) and he raised Paul to a higher level than himself (Acts 11:26; 13:50).

6. Paul was a great leader because he was able to train other leaders to join him in ministry. Paul told Timothy to take the things he had taught him and pass them on to faithful people, who would be able to train others (2 Timothy 2:1–2). Here we have four generations of leadership training – Paul, Timothy, faithful people and then others!

In describing the function of church leadership, Paul says that each ministry has been given to *'equip the saints to do the work of the ministry'* (Ephesians 4:11–12).

1. **Apostles** aren't just called to break new ground and establish new churches. They are to teach and equip God's people so that they also have a mission from God to reach out to the world around them and help people lay spiritual foundations in their lives.

2. **Prophets** aren't just called to prophesy. They are to teach and equip God's people to hear God for themselves and live their daily lives in tune with the Holy Spirit.

3. **Evangelists** aren't just called to do all the evangelizing. They are to teach and equip God's people to share their faith and be effective soul-winners.

4. **Pastors** aren't just called to do all the caring. They are to teach and equip God's people to love and minister to one another.

5. **Teachers** aren't just called to do all the teaching. They are to teach and equip God's people to study, interpret and apply God's Word to their own lives.

Believers who are equipped in these five key areas of ministry will be on their way to becoming mature disciples of Jesus!

Looking at the above few examples, we can clearly see that the biblical pattern of leadership is that God constantly works through a leadership team and He requires those leaders to mobilize others into ministry.

What is your personal style of leadership?

Our Mandate – Make Disciples!

Although Jesus loved everybody and ministered regularly to the multitudes, He recognized that it was only through committed disciples that the Church would be built. Therefore, He invested His prime time into a small group of twelve people He had chosen to be His disciples. Jesus mentored and trained them personally for three and a half years. Before He ascended to heaven, He told these disciples, 'Go and make disciples of all nations, teaching them to observe everything I have commanded you.'

Jesus gave His team of twelve disciples a mission and a mandate. The mission was to take the gospel to the ends of the earth. The mandate was to take those who responded and make them into disciples. This begins with conversion and then involves a lifelong process of teaching and training them in the lifestyle of the kingdom. The twelve apostles obeyed Jesus' mandate by giving themselves to proclaiming the gospel and making disciples.

Making disciples must be the priority of the Church of Jesus Christ – not just holding meetings, singing songs or teaching sermons. The focus of the leaders of the church must be on reproducing fully devoted and fully functioning disciples of Jesus Christ. Every program and ministry must work towards this end. This is what we will be accountable for when Jesus returns – how many, and what kind of, disciples did we produce for the benefit of God's kingdom?

Every Christian is to be a disciple and every disciple should make other disciples. The disciple-making process will last until Jesus returns.

What is Discipling?

A disciple is a follower of Jesus Christ. It refers to a student, a learner and someone who is dedicated to becoming like Jesus in every aspect of life.

Bill Hull defines discipling as:

> 'The intentional training of disciples, with accountability, on the basis of loving relationships.'[2]

Intentional means there needs to be a planned strategy, including a method and a model. **Training** implies a prescribed course of study and a specific process that people go through. **With accountability** is important because people need help to keep their commitments. **Loving relationships** provide the loving, supportive environment in which disciple-making can best take place.

What Kind of Disciples Do We Want?

God wants each Christian to be a fervent disciple or follower of Jesus Christ. To be fervent means to be passionate, zealous, earnest, enthusiastic, fiery, ardent, intense, ablaze, burning and hot. This is in stark contrast to lukewarmness, complacency, lethargy and indifference (Matthew 3:11–12; John 2:17; Acts 2:3–4; Romans 12:11; Colossians 3:23; Titus 2:14).

The last church Jesus spoke to, through John the apostle, was Laodecia (Revelation 3:14–22). This was a very large, wealthy and powerful church. It was rich, abounding in goods, and saw itself as in need of nothing. It was thoroughly satisfied with its own progress and prosperity, but in the eyes of the Lord it was poor, miserable, blind and naked because it was lukewarm and lacking in spiritual fervor.

In contrast, the believers at Antioch were so fervent in their zeal for God that they were the first ones to be called 'Christians' – those belonging to or like Jesus Christ (Acts 11:26). This was an indication of the quality of their discipleship.

We desire to be fervent followers of Jesus Christ, demonstrating our whole-hearted devotion by praying, worshipping, loving and serving with a spirit of fervency. These are the kind of disciples God wants us to be and to raise up.

Disciple-Making Through Cell Groups

A Cell Group is one of the best places for disciple-making to take place. It is a place where Christians can grow together to become fervent followers of Jesus Christ through the process of discipling, teaching and mentoring.

How Do We Make Disciples?

Jesus modeled a disciple-making process with His small group of twelve disciples. His strategy had four basic components, which are the essentials of effective disciple making today. They are outlined in the following diagram:

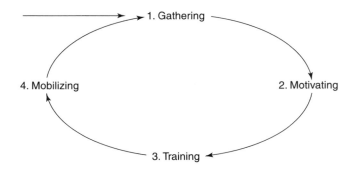

Let's look at these four steps in more detail especially as they apply to a Cell Group:

1. **Gathering**. This is the first step. You start by seeking to gather people who are potential disciples, then you develop quality relationships with the people in your group. This is done by expressing interest in their personal and family life through asking questions and active listening. Be warm towards them through sensitivity and kindness. Avoid sarcasm, criticism, defensiveness, correction or advice giving. Get to know them – how long they've been Christians, their level of spiritual maturity, their family backgrounds, their careers, their church involvement, their hobbies and their personal interests, friendships, needs, hurts, dreams, etc.

2. **Motivating**. This is the second step. Help people to see what they can become and then lead them to make a commitment to achieving that God-given potential.

   If you are a Cell Group Leader, you must be an example of a fervent disciple. Be totally committed to your own personal spiritual growth. Be an example of what a disciple should be and be open and real about your own struggles and victories. These kinds of things are tremendous motivators.

   You must motivate people to lay hold of God's purpose for their life and to commit themselves to achieving their personal destiny. You must also give them a passionate vision for the Church of Jesus Christ and an understanding of how they can contribute to it. Help them develop their potential in God through encouragement, counsel, affirmation and challenge.

3. **Training**. This is the third step in the process. Equip people to live successfully and to develop an effective ministry.

   The Cell Group Leader must give instruction about the Christian life. Teach people the commands of Jesus and the values of the Kingdom of God. Teach them the basic principles of Christian living and help them apply the Word of God to their lives.

A good leader determines where people are at right now in their spiritual journey and seeks to move them to where they need to be via the next step. We can't disciple people until we determine their point of need and what type of equipping is required to move them forward. The Cell Group Leader must have as their major objective the maturity and personal growth of each member of their group. Helping people to grow spiritually is the focus.

4. **Mobilizing**. This is the fourth step. You delegate and release them into significant ministry. Provide opportunities for practical implementation of what has been taught. Your goal is to mobilize people to actively serve others with their gifts and abilities on a regular basis.

It's not enough just to gather, motivate and train people. We must put them to work. People need outlet and challenge. Believe that God has a part for each person to play, then help them find their place and begin to function. People must keep learning, but they can't stay in school forever. They need to do something with what they have been taught and make a contribution to the world! The Cell Group Leader must intentionally seek to help the people in the group become active in Christian service.

This is not the last step. The act of gathering becomes a regular part of the disciple-making process as you gather those you are discipling together for feedback and further training. Then the cycle continues with further motivating, training and mobilizing. Throughout the process you need to ask questions and give appropriate feedback to coach them in their personal and ministry development.

Helping people become fervent followers of Jesus Christ is a process of spiritual growth that takes time. It is like helping a baby to grow and to develop until he or she becomes a mature person who is able to contribute to society.

Although this process includes one-to-one relationships, it takes place best within a small group context. A small group creates an environment of mutual support, ministry, accountability and training. Small groups also enable inter-action, discussion and application of practical Christian life to occur in a safe, open environment. This is the New Testament model. Jesus discipled twelve people in a small group (Mark 3:14; Matthew 10:5–42).

Disciple making requires the work of the Holy Spirit, obedience, intimacy with Christ, life experiences and accountable relationships. A Cell Group Leader cannot **cause** spiritual growth but he or she can create an environment that promotes and facilitates such growth.

Share the Ministry

Church leaders are called to equip or prepare the saints for the work of the ministry. Processes must be developed to enable people to discover their spiritual gifts, abilities, personality and passion. Then people need to be given ministry opportunities in which to serve. Once placed, they need continual encouragement, coaching and resources in order to be effective.

As leaders, we must not hold on to ministry for ourselves, rather we must release it and share it with others. When it comes to ministry in the church, we must have an **abundance mentality** that sees that there is more work to be done than we can do ourselves. In fact, the impact of the church will only be as large as the amount of kingdom workers we are able to mobilize.[3]

We must learn to delegate effectively. The art of delegation is one of the most powerful tools leaders have. It increases their individual productivity as well as the productivity of their ministry. Leaders who can't or won't delegate create a bottleneck to growth and development. The other benefit of delegation is that it increases the initiative of the people within the church, because it gives them a chance to grow and succeed.

Delegation can be defined as 'the process of identifying your ministry responsibilities and assigning portions of your work to others, so that the workers become fulfilled and the work is accomplished.' Your primary motivation in delegation is not just getting rid of work you don't want to do – it is **developing people!**

One of the greatest joys of a leader is to see others grow into effective ministry. Leaders should rejoice when those they train do well and even surpass their own effectiveness. Jesus told His disciples that they would do greater works than He had done. Elisha had a double portion of Elijah's anointing and he did twice as many miracles. This kind of attitude requires an internal security that finds identity in who you are, not in what you do or the position you hold. Attitudes of insecurity, jealousy and competition merely hinder the growth of the church and the development of people.

Delegation is an important part of any leader's success, yet so many leaders fail to delegate effectively. This may be due to a lack of confidence in others, a lack of training ability, an unwillingness to give up the task because of personal enjoyment, inability to find someone to delegate to, a lack of time to train, or a belief that no one else can do it as well.

Church leaders must begin to believe in people, then give them opportunity to learn and develop in ministry areas. It will take time, patience and training, but delegation will multiply the ministry and develop people like nothing else.

Why do people get involved in ministry? Sometimes, unfortunately, people volunteer because they are pressured, made to feel guilty, pushed, manipulated or don't know when or how to say 'No'. This creates a situation that is detrimental for both the individual and the ministry.

Where people are encouraged to volunteer freely in areas of interest and gifting, there is a much greater possibility of long-term effective ministry. John Maxwell, in his *Lay Ministry* training seminar, says that people usually volunteer because of one or more of the following reasons.[4]

1. People want to be needed. This is one of the most basic human needs.

2. People want to help others.

3. People want to make a difference. People don't want a blank tombstone. They desperately want to be part of something greater than themselves.

4. People want to learn new skills and improve the skills they already have. Otherwise, life turns out to be a survival only – a maintenance system.

5. People want a sense of belonging and acceptance. It's terrible to be an outsider, unaccepted, unwanted.

6. People like to feel good about themselves. They like affirmation.

7. People want recognition.

8. Christians want to mature in their faith and share their God-given talents. God creates in us a natural desire for growth.

9. People want to keep from being lonely. There is nothing worse in the world than genuine loneliness.

10. People want to support causes they believe in.

As leaders, we need to understand why people get involved in ministry, then seek to motivate and assist them to a place of ongoing fruitfulness and fulfillment.

Becoming an Effective Mentor or Coach

Another word for discipling is the word 'mentoring'. Every Christian needs three kinds of mentoring relationships: [5]

1. A Paul – someone who is more mature than them who can help them grow and develop further as a Christian.

2. A Barnabas – someone who is a peer who can also inspire and teach them.

3. A Timothy – someone who is less mature than them to whom they can be a mentor and be an encouragement to.

Each of us should find many different mentors, in each of the above three categories, who can help us along our spiritual journey.

A modern day example of a mentor is a coach. In fact, every church leader needs to take on the role of a coach as he or she leads their area of ministry. Coaching is the hands-on process of helping someone else succeed. It includes helping them improve their own ministry effectiveness, but also involves helping them grow as a person so they reach their God-given potential, and helping them to work together effectively with others.

Good coaches perform a number of important tasks for the team:

1. They recruit people to the team.
2. They establish challenging but attainable goals and priorities.
3. They inspire the team to maximum performance.
4. They design a strategy for the team.
5. They conduct team practices or training sessions.
6. They develop the skills of the individual as well as those of the team working together.
7. They affirm team players consistently by reinforcing positive behavior.
8. They correct team players when necessary by discouraging negative behavior.
9. They cultivate a team spirit and winning environment.
10. They value each person's unique contribution through realizing that every player can do something better than anyone else.
11. They build group or team cohesiveness.
12. They plan regular celebrations of victories and successes.

Effective coaching requires building a healthy relationship with the person or team member and showing interest their family and personal life. It also requires helping them to be effective in their ministry area through setting goals, skill training and personal development.

Where Have All the Leaders Gone?

The Church desperately needs people with the gift of leadership to emerge and to use their gift to help the Church to grow and change (Romans 12:6–8).

Effective leaders accomplish a number of important tasks for the church:

1. They receive a **vision** from God for their church or ministry.

2. They help define and model biblical **core values** for the ministry.

3. They develop a **strategic plan** for making the vision a reality that includes ministry **priorities, goals and objectives.**

4. They **gather and motivate people** to own the vision and contribute to its accomplishment.

5. They provide regular **training and equipping** to help people develop excellence in their ministry.

6. They gather and apply **resources** to the vision.

7. They develop **systems, structures and programs** that serve to implement the vision.

8. They regularly **evaluate and make adjustments** to ensure that the ministry stays on course.

More Workers, Please!

The harvest is huge. The need is great. What we need are more willing workers to get involved in the work of the ministry. Let's pray and believe for God to use the leaders of today's church to disciple many people into effective ministry.

Jesus did not suggest that we pray for a bigger task or a larger harvest field, as if the Great Commission is not challenging enough. He told us to pray for more laborers – more people who will take up the challenge of working for the expansion of the kingdom (Matthew 9:36–38).

People development takes time. John Maxwell, says,

'It is better to train ten people to work than to do the work of ten people, but it is harder.'

He goes on to say,

'If you can't work any harder, your future growth in production will be determined by your ability to work through other people. A great leader develops a team of people who increase production. The result? The leader's influence and effectiveness begin to multiply (working through others) instead of adding (working by oneself).'

Leadership development is the key issue for the ongoing health and growth of any ministry. The mission of the Church is huge and it requires everyone to be involved in ministry. Our job as leaders is to train others to commit their lives to the purposes of God.

All of us must seek to pass on to others what we know for their benefit. Be a disciple maker! Teach others what you know and what you have learned by experience. You are an influencer of others. Be an example, a model and a mentor.

As each person begins to contribute, their life will be more fulfilled and fruitful. Together, we can reach out and impact communities, cities and nations for the kingdom of God. Together, let's make a **Leadership Shift** so the Church can make a bigger difference in our world to the glory of God.

Notes

1. This story is found in Chapter 1 and the analogy of the difference between a **shepherd** and a **rancher** is developed in Chapter 6 (Grand Rapids, Michigan: Baker Book House, 1993). This book establishes the fact that many churches never grow beyond 200 because of the leadership style of the Senior Pastor.

2. This quote is from Bill Hull's book, *The Disciple Making Church* (Tarrytown, New York: Fleming H. Revell, 1990, p.32). Bill Hull also has another good book entitled *The Disciple Making Pastor*.

3. John Maxwell's book, *Developing the Leaders Around You*, shows the extreme importance of building a quality leadership team that will multiply the ministry of the church (Nashville, Tennessee: Thomas Nelson Publishers, 1995).

4. The *Lay Ministry* training seminar by John Maxwell (San Diego, California: INJOY, 1989) is an outstanding resource to help church leaders make this important **Leadership Shift**.

5. This concept is taken from the book, *The Seven Promises of a Promise Keeper* (Colorado Springs, Colorado: Focus on the Family Publishers, 1994).

Personal Action Plan

Here are some ideas to help you make a personal **Leadership Shift**:

1. Determine to share what God has given you. Take the things that you are good at, the things that you know and the things you have experienced and share them with someone else who could benefit from them.

2. If you have children of your own, think about ways that you can train and develop their potential.

3. Ask one of your church leaders if you can help them in a voluntary capacity. Make a commitment to serve them and help release them to do what only they can do.

4. Get involved in helping to establish new Christians in the church.

5. Make a list of areas you would like to grow in, then find someone who can mentor you in each area. Regular personal contact with a mentor is ideal, but you can also be mentored through a book, a tape or just a brief lunch with someone who can give you some keys to growing in a particular area of your life.

6. Help out in your church's children's or youth ministry. Learn to teach and train others.

7. Sign up to be an assistant coach of a sports team and get some experience bringing out the best in others.

8. Think about people who have had a positive influence on your life. Analyze how and why they influenced you and determine to do the same to others.

9. Determine to give away everything you can to benefit others.

Church Action Plan

Here are some ideas to help your church make a **Leadership Shift**:

1. Answer the following questions for each ministry in the church:

   (a) What does the future of this ministry look like? How big will it be? How much will you be able to do and how many people will you be able to reach or care for?

   (b) Produce an organizational outline of leaders, including assistants.

   (c) Where are the leadership gaps?

   (d) Which positions are the highest priority for apprenticeship training?

   (e) Where are the biggest training needs?

   (f) Do you have a program in place to meet them?

   (g) If not, what could be done to meet this training need?

2. As a church leader, determine what areas of ministry you could delegate to others. To do this, do the following:

   (a) List all your current activities.

   (b) Combine tasks into natural groupings.

   (c) Eliminate unnecessary activities. Ask yourself, 'Does this need to be done?'

   (d) Circle tasks someone else could do.

   (e) Put an asterisk by each one that **only** you can do. These should only be a few tasks!

   (f) List other important activities you should be doing.

   (g) Choose at least five tasks from the list and consider who you could delegate each task to and when.

   (h) Do it!

3. Conduct some training sessions for church leaders in the area of coaching and mentoring. You may want to use an external church consultant.

4.   Require church leaders to reproduce themselves and raise up other leaders in their area of ministry.

5.   Start another church meeting and mobilize a whole new group of volunteers.

6.   Require all Cell Group leaders to train an assistant who can become a leader when the group multiplies.

7.   Start a leadership training program within your church to raise up more leaders and to equip current leaders.

SHIFT 5

A Ministry Shift
from consumers to contributors

*'Each one should use whatever gift he has received
to serve others, faithfully administering God's grace
in its various forms.'*

(1 Peter 4:10)

Becoming a Mobilized Community

A Ministry Shift

We have looked at the importance of making a **Leadership Shift**, which requires church leaders to shift their focus from being ministers to becoming equippers. In the church, everyone is a minister and the role of the leadership is to equip each person for effective ministry.

The next strategic shift is a **Ministry Shift**. This shift requires each Christian to shift their focus from being a **consumer** to becoming a **contributor** in the kingdom of God. Only as each Christian gets actively involved will we see the change necessary for the Church to become a force in the world.

I believe that people are looking for significance in life and this is found by giving their lives to a cause beyond themselves. God has a vision, a dream and a destiny for each individual person and this includes a significant contribution to the local church.

The **First Reformation** put the Bible back in the hands of believers, but it didn't go far enough. It's time for a **Second Reformation**, where the work of the ministry is returned to every Christian.

God's Plan for You

A number of years ago, gospel singer Michael W. Smith had a hit song called *Place in This World*. The message of this song touches on one of the core needs that every human being is born with – to find their place in the world. We have a deep desire for our lives to have a sense of purpose and meaning. Each one of us wants to know the answers to the questions, 'Who am I?' and 'What am I here for?' Thankfully, the Bible teaches us that God has a plan and a purpose for each person.

In Matthew 4:18–22, we see Jesus calling the first disciples: two sets of brothers, Simon and Andrew, as well as James and John. Let's look at some important lessons from this story.[1]

God Wants You on His Team

Jesus calls people to be a part of the work that He is doing. God is into teams. God Himself is a team of three Persons working together and sharing ministry. The very nature of God reflects His desire for us to work together with one another and share the ministry of the Church.

Jesus came to earth to save us from our sin and to make a way for us to be restored to a right relationship with God. He also came to build His Church – a group of people filled with the power of the Holy Spirit who would reach out and change their world. He said,

> *'I will build my church and the gates of hell will not prevail against it.'*   (Matthew 16:18)

However, Jesus decided that He was not going to do all the work Himself, even though He could have accomplished it this way. He chose people to be on His team and carry out His work. Jesus selected twelve disciples to share the ministry with Him and later told them to do the same with others.

God is in the recruiting business. History is full of examples of ordinary people that God chose and then used for extraordinary tasks. Think of Abraham, Moses, David, Mary and Peter to name just a few.

God is doing a great work and He has selected you to be on His team. Amazing! In His Church, every Christian is supposed to be on the team. Every member is a minister and has a position to fill and a job to do. The word 'ministry', which is used throughout the New Testament, is the Greek word *diakonos* which simply means 'one who serves'. It is not a special office, but rather a special function. Ministry is simply an act of service given in Jesus' name.

Jesus doesn't just want church attenders or even church members. He wants people who are actively involved with His work. God wants to make use of your time, resources and talents for the expansion of His kingdom on earth.

What a wonderful opportunity God has given us to be players on His team. When we contribute, we find fulfillment and we begin to grow. We experience the joy and privilege of being a co-builder of God's eternal kingdom.

The Bible teaches us a number of very important things concerning each Christian's role in the Church of Jesus Christ.[2] Let's look at four important truths.

1. You are a part of the 'Body of Christ'

Every true believer is part of the Church, which is the Body of Christ (Romans 12:5; 1 Corinthians 12:27). There is one body, but many members in each local church.

God places people in His body as He pleases (1 Corinthians 12:18, 24, 28; Ephesians 4:7, 11). We must accept God's choosing and be content. Don't compare yourself with others, because this just leads to competition or envy. Don't think yourself too lowly through feelings of inferiority (1 Corinthians 12:15–16); don't think too highly of yourself through feelings of superiority (1 Corinthians 12:21). We need each other. There are no unnecessary members or especially important members.

2. You have been given a spiritual gift

You have received spiritual gifts so that you can serve other people and so that the Church might be built (1 Peter 4:10). Everyone has at least one gift. Paul says,

> *'To **each one** the manifestation of the Spirit is given for the common good.'*   (1 Corinthians 12:7, 11)

Peter Wagner defines a spiritual gift as a 'special ability or attribute given by the Holy Spirit to each member, enabling them to minister to the needs of Christ's body, the Church.'[3] There are over twenty different gifts mentioned in the New Testament and each of these has a wide variety of expressions and variations.

God gives spiritual gifts as He pleases or chooses. Paul says that they are given as God wills or determines (1 Corinthians 12:11; Ephesians 4:7).

You may ask, 'How do I know what my gift is?' You should first explore the possibilities, then experiment with as many as you can. Look for needs and try to meet them. Find opportunities and make yourself available. Initially you may discover what gifts you don't have. Examine your own feelings and gauge your effectiveness. Gifts are task-orientated, so we should expect them to work and produce a positive result. Confirmation from other people is also important.

In addition to spiritual gifts, we all have strong desires and interests that God uses to direct us into areas of service that fit us best. You may prefer to work with things, people or information. You may enjoy working with different age groups of people. You have a unique personality with special concerns, interests and passions that are usually tied in to your spiritual gifts.[4]

3. You have a specific job to do

Not only is every Christian a part of the Body of Christ with unique spiritual gifts, they also have a special function, a task to complete and a job to do based on the gifts they have. In our physical body, the eye is a part of the body, it has the gift of sight and its job is to observe, watch and see what is happening near the body.

We have each received a gift, so we should use it to minister to one another (1 Peter 4:10). Get involved in various aspects of the ministry of the church. You don't need an official position or a title to serve others. There are many incredible ministries to be involved in and you don't need a seminary degree to start. **Availability** is just as important as **ability**.

Remember that God's heart and focus is people. All true ministry must be focused ultimately on helping people through giving, sharing, loving, encouraging and serving.

Jesus had to teach this to the disciples. The disciples scolded a group of children for interrupting Jesus' ministry (Matthew 19:13–15). Jesus had to rebuke the disciples and explain that children were near to His heart and an important part of the kingdom of God.

When five thousand people grew tired and hungry after gathering to hear Jesus speak, the disciples asked Jesus if they should send them away (Matthew 14:15–21). Jesus made the disciples care for them and meet their needs. When a blind man began shouting to get Jesus' attention, the disciples rebuked him and told him to be quiet (Luke 18:35–43). Once again, Jesus had to teach them that He was interested in the poor and needy.

The disciples started with a focus on self. They were more caught up with their own ministry and their position in the kingdom than having a heart to serve people. They had to learn to look beyond themselves. Jesus had to teach them that the foundation of all ministry is serving people! All gifts and ministries in the church are simply tools to help us serve. Our focus must be people, not gifts or ministry!

Jesus was the prime example of a servant. He had all the gifts and all the ministries, yet note how He summarized His ministry. He said,

> *'The Son of man came not to be served, but to serve, and give His life a ransom for many.'*

This startling statement came in the context of a conversation with the mother of James and John, who was seeking position, power and authority for her sons (Matthew 20:20–28).

In John 13:1–17, we have the record of Jesus washing the disciples' feet. Washing the dusty feet of guests was the role of the servant of the house. Jesus was teaching His disciples to serve others and not to be focused on themselves. Our attitude should not be, 'Here I am, serve me' but rather, 'There you are, let me serve you.' God wants us to be givers, not takers. In serving others, we are serving God. If we do not serve others, we are not serving God.

Serving is at the very heart of Christianity and Christlikeness. Let's serve one another with the gifts we have been given. Have a change of attitude, perspective and focus. Wake up every morning with the attitude, 'I am a servant.' Do everything as unto the Lord, to please Him. Take the initiative, be willing, be faithful, be diligent, be joyful and be obedient.

4. The growth of the body is dependent on your contribution

The church is incomplete and ineffective without everyone's gift. The body only grows as each member contributes by doing their work (Ephesians 4:15–16). If an individual member is not using their gift or doing their job, the whole body is hindered in its growth and its effectiveness. On the other hand, when each person discovers and uses their gifts, the whole body benefits.

Imagine gifts under a Christmas tree, all carefully wrapped yet unopened. Never enjoyed, never experienced, never appreciated and never able to benefit others. The church was not designed to be a house full of unwrapped gifts. God expects you to open them up and use them. Every gift, no matter how small, should be used.

5. God sees what you can become, not just what you are now

Jesus said to the first disciples that He called, *'I will make you fishers of men'* (Matthew 4:19). He saw not just what they were, but what they could become.

The disciples were unexpected choices for Jesus' team and unlikely heroes but Jesus focused on their potential, not their past. He called them from where they were and gave them hope and a vision to do something significant for God.

Note Jesus' attitude towards Simon Peter (John 1:40–42). Jesus told Simon that he would become Peter (a name which means 'a rock'). Simon was anything but a rock. He was impulsive and unstable. Jesus named him Peter, not for what he was, but for what, by God's grace, he would become. Through the years, Peter had some great moments and some low moments, but eventually he became a pillar and a foundational leader of the early Church (Acts 2:14; Galatians 2:9).

When God appeared to Gideon, who was hiding from his enemies, He said, *'The Lord is with you, mighty warrior!'* God definitely saw Gideon differently than the way he saw himself (Judges 6:11–12).

John Maxwell, in his *Lay Ministry* training seminar, says,

'Man surveys the crowd and evaluates it by what they were (the past) and what they are (the present). God surveys the crowd and evaluates it by what they are (the present) and what they can become (the future).'

History is filled with examples of people who had tremendous potential that were initially overlooked. Einstein couldn't speak until he was four years of age, or read until the age of seven. One of Beethoven's early piano teachers said that he was hopeless as a composer. Thomas Edison's teacher said he was so stupid he'd never learn anything. Walt Disney was fired by a newspaper editor for not being creative enough and for not having enough new ideas. Ray Kroc at the age of fifty-seven began a hamburger shop in the midst of a recession, against advice from experienced people. It's now known all over the world as McDonalds.

In the same way, it is so easy to miss the tremendous potential resident in the lives of believers who have been called by God to have a significant place in His kingdom.

Think about Peter, James, John and Andrew. They impacted their world as thousands of people came into the Church. Religious and political institutions were shaken. People were healed and lives were transformed. Books were written that live on today, almost two thousand years later. Yet they were just ordinary fishermen, untrained and unskilled.

We tend to become what those closest to us believe we could be. My life is filled with people who saw what I could become and encouraged me to develop my potential.

What does God see as He looks at your church today? He sees book writers, song writers, singers, creative artists, politicians, business owners, millionaires, pastors, church planting teams, prophetic ministries, preachers, youth leaders, inventors, intercessors, healing ministries, administrators, small group leaders, radio ministries, evangelists, teachers, counselors, missionaries, children's workers, computer programmers, scientists, doctors, tradesmen and servant ministries. Even people yet to be saved have a great destiny in God.

Believe in people and help them to believe in themselves. John Maxwell goes on to say,

> 'It is important that the people believe in their leader, but it is more important that the leader believes in his people.'

People often rise to the level of the encouragement they

receive. Church leaders need to be the greatest cheerleaders for people in their congregation.

Yes, you can have a **significant** ministry. It may not be **prominent**, but you can make a difference in someone's life. You can do something to build God's kingdom. You have potential to do great things for God.

God is Committed to Helping You Succeed

Jesus was willing to help the disciples reach their potential. He said, *'I will make you fishers of men.'* He committed His time to work with them, to give them responsibility, to train them, to encourage them and to develop their potential. He would never give up on them, despite their failures. He would pray for them and support them all the way through. His whole life focus was serving them and helping them to be effective.

What God has placed within you, He will draw out. You are His workmanship. As a team member, He will spend time with you to help you find your place and to be the very best you can be.

The leaders of the church need to be committed to do everything they can to care for their people and to help them become effective ministers for Jesus Christ. That's their job! Leaders exist to gather, motivate, train and mobilize Christians into service for God.

You Have to Make a Commitment to Him

God will do His part if we do ours. Jesus called to His potential disciples, 'Come, follow Me.' They had to let go of what was in their hand and follow Him. They had to come out of the crowd and on to Jesus' team. Jesus was limited in what He could do with them without their commitment. Jesus gave His disciples a challenge to become active in ministry and a chance to be involved.

We too, must step across the line. Times of significant change come at the point of commitment. We must choose to commit ourselves to Jesus and to His team, the Church.

You Will Be Rewarded for the Work That You Do

Those first disciples followed Jesus and literally laid down their lives as they worked to build the Church. Yet Jesus promised them great reward, in both this life and the life to come.

At the return of Christ, we too will be rewarded according to our works (Matthew 16:27). Everything we do should be as service unto Christ (Colossians 3:23–24; Hebrews 6:10–12).

We know that we are saved by grace, through faith, not by works, lest anyone should boast. Salvation is a gift of God. However, we are His workmanship, created for **good works** (Ephesians 2:8–10). This is God's purpose for us. We weren't saved just to go to heaven, but to serve God's purpose right here, right now.

The gospel message is 'Live and Do' (faith-righteousness), not 'Do and live' (self-righteousness). We are justified by faith (Romans 1:17), but faith that is active and alive must be demonstrated by good works (James 2:14–26).

What are good works? Good works are something done for the benefit of others, motivated by love and a servant spirit. When we serve others, we serve God. Every time we give even a cup of water to someone in Jesus' name He notices it. He writes it down and He remembers it. He also accepts it as to Himself and He will reward it. Even insignificant love gifts are great in His eyes. The main distinction between the sheep and the goats in Jesus' parable was the practical service they did or didn't do as unto Him (Matthew 25:31–46).

In the parable of the talents, the servants were rewarded for diligence and faithfulness, not for the amount they were given (Matthew 25:14–30). In the same way, our future rewards will be given not for position, title, gift or function, but according to what we've done with what we've been given.

The quality and motivation of that we do will be tested by fire (1 Corinthians 3:10–15). This should give us a healthy fear of God and cause us to place our priority on eternal things and the work of the kingdom.

Understanding How God's Team Works

A modern day illustration of this concept is a basketball team. God is the owner, the pastor is the coach and the church members are the players on the team. No matter how important the owner and the coach are, without the players, there is no team![5]

Imagine the following three scenes in a basketball game:

1. The coach plays alone

Imagine the players on a basketball team staying on the bench while they send the coach out to do all the work. The result? Ineffectiveness and a burnt out coach! Any team that did this would be seen as crazy, yet many churches do it all the time. They expect the pastor to do all the work while they cheer him or her on. No wonder so many ministers burn out and give up.

The coach cannot play alone. He needs the team. The pastor is the coach. He is to equip the congregation for the work of ministry.

2. The players stay in the huddle

Imagine a team of basketball players getting off the bench and on to the court but then staying in the huddle for the entire game.

Any team that did this would be foolish, yet often church can be just like this. Every Sunday we get in a 'holy huddle' and talk about all the things we're going to do. We look at the 'play-book' and take notes, but do we ever do anything about it? We may think that this is ministry, but coming to church is not our ministry. Real ministry begins at the end of the church meeting.

You may have seen game zone places where you can get on a motorbike and ride, while you look at the video screen in front of you. You go through all the emotions and feelings, but when you get off, you haven't been anywhere. In the same way, church meetings can be a type of **simulation exercise**. This is not to, in any way, underestimate what God can do when we gather together, but the danger is that we can live in a fantasy world where we think that, because we have talked and sung about it, we're really doing it.

The huddle is important, but it only exists to get us ready for the real game, where each of us takes our place and begins to contribute.

3. The players argue instead of lining up

Imagine the basketball team finally getting out of the huddle and on to the court and then starting to fight over the uniform colors, the play that's been called, or the position they've been asked to play.

Any team that acted like this would be seen as foolish, but some churches are just like this. Some Christians fight over insignificant things and get focused on themselves, while forgetting that there's a game to be played and a battle to be won. No wonder the saints aren't winning by as much as they should be!

Half Time

Praise God for half time! Church leaders and people are realizing that something has to change if the Church is going to be more effective. Pastors (the coaches) are starting to apologize for doing the entire ministry themselves and for not equipping people. Christians (the players) are realizing that they need to get off the bench and start getting involved in the game. Just maybe, we can come out in the second half and turn the situation around. After all, God has called us to be winners.

Ministry in Cell Groups

A Cell Group is an ideal place for people to begin to serve others. As people develop confidence and gain experience, they can minister in other church gatherings. A Cell Group should be a **Ministry Group** where Christians can develop and use their God-given gifts and abilities to help others.

Spiritual Employment

The Church is God's **Employment Service**. We are to ensure that each person discovers and uses their gifts and abilities to help others. There is to be no spiritual unemployment in the kingdom of heaven!

If you are a church leader, you are an employment agent! You are to be actively involved in recruiting people for the work of the ministry. God wants you to motivate people to a life of purpose and then help them find opportunities for ministry.

To be an effective mobilizer of others, you need to:

1. Be aware of the different spiritual gifts or ministries.

2. Be aware of any current ministry opportunities.

3. Discover each person's passion, package of God-given gifts, and personality. Discern which ministry will best match the way God has made them and help them begin.

4. Understand the process of ministry development. See potential in people. Look beyond where they are now to what they can become with God's help. Begin where they are and call them to a greater level of commitment and involvement.

What a privilege to be co-workers with God in building His Church and extending His kingdom!

Cell Group Goals

Cell Group Leaders need to help each person in their group develop ministry in three areas.

1. Ministry in the Cell Group

The first goal is to see each person ministering or contributing to the Cell Group. A Cell Group is the best place for people to begin to serve others. Here is where they can develop confidence and gain experience in a warm and safe environment.

People feel fulfilled and a part of something when they are able to contribute. Leaders do not need to do all the leading.

One person does not possess all the gifts, energy and time to do everything needed by the group. As a leader, you are responsible to find out people's gifts and abilities and then involve them in those areas.

Here are some ways to develop people's ministry in the Cell Group:

- Involve people in various aspects of the Cell Group meeting. This could include prayer, song leading, discussion, games, supper, children's program, visitor follow up, meals for those in need, etc.

- Don't force people to do something they're not comfortable with. Nobody can do everything, but everybody can do something.

- Praise and acknowledge those people working behind the scenes.

- Model things by showing them how to do it, and then delegate by giving them an opportunity to minister.

- Give constructive feedback and appropriate training.

- Direct what is happening, without appearing to control.

Team ministry provides a great deal of variety, and people will be more committed to something they are personally involved in.

2. Ministry in the Church

Your second goal is to see each person ministering or contributing to the church. Most churches need volunteers in each area of ministry, so encourage the members of your Cell Group get involved.

Your entire Cell Group can also contribute to the wider ministry of the church on a regular basis. In fact, Cell Groups can take on much of the ministry of the church and help avoid the continual addition of more and more departments and ministries that tend to compete for resources.[6]

There is so much to be done. No church that I know of has enough volunteers. Usually, there is a shortage. The following humorous story illustrates this:

There were once four people named Everybody, Somebody, Anybody and Nobody. There was an important job to be done and Everybody was sure that Somebody would do it. Anybody could have done it, but Nobody did it. Now Somebody got angry about that because it was Everybody's job. Everybody thought Anybody could do it, but Nobody realized that Everybody wouldn't do it. It ended up that Everybody blamed Somebody when Nobody did what Anybody could have done. When there is no commitment, Nobody does it!

3. Ministry to the world

Your third goal is to see each person contributing to society in a positive way. This may be in their neighborhood, their school or their workplace. God wants each Christian to use their gifts and abilities to help others outside the church. We each have a ministry to the world to be salt and light (Matthew 5:13–16). We do this through good works and our witness for Jesus Christ.

Each Cell Group Leader needs to encourage the members of their group to aim for excellence in every area of their life, then use their influence for sharing the good news of Jesus Christ.

As each person becomes a contributor, their life will be more fulfilled and fruitful. Spiritual maturity is not measured by how long a person has been a Christian, by how many times a person attends church, or by the amount of biblical knowledge they may have. It is measured by the character of a person's life and the contribution that they make to help other people.

We grow by putting into practice what we hear and know. We need to become doers of the word and not hearers only (James 1:22–25). Active ministry or service promotes personal growth and is pleasing to God. It unleashes the power of the Holy Spirit and multiplies the potential of the Church.

A Ministry Check-up

Most churches are made up of four different groups of people:

1. Christians who have made no commitment to the church, but simply attend on an occasional basis. God calls to them to step out of the crowd and make a commitment to be partners in the ministry of the church. Don't be just a consumer, become a contributor. God wants every Christian joined to a local church where they can grow and contribute (Acts 2:41, 47). Those who are planted in God's house will flourish and be fruitful (Psalm 92:12–14). Commitment is a positive thing.

2. Christians who are hurting and who are in the process of being restored or healed before they function. The Church is to be a loving community where people who are wounded can receive care and help. Once hurting people become emotionally healthy and spiritually fit, they can get involved in ministry once again.

3. Christians who are committed to a church, but are not yet functioning. This may be because they either don't know their gift, or aren't using it for some reason. God calls these believers to get involved in a ministry. The church needs more ministers, not just more members. Don't be an onlooker. Get involved in ministry.

    Non-functioning members may be in one of three situations:

    (a) Those who are uninterested because of complacency. They are happy to let others do all the work. This is a dangerous condition and invites Jesus' rebuke. God hates lukewarmness, in fact, it makes Him sick (Revelation 3:14–22).

    (b) Those who are frustrated because they know their gift, but are not functioning, maybe through lack of opportunity. Speak to your pastor or church leader and see where you can become involved.

    (c) Those who are ignorant, because they don't know their spiritual gifts, but would like to. They need to discern and develop their gifts.

4. Christians who are committed to the church and who are actively using their gifts to serve others. These

Christians need to continue to develop their gifts and look to train someone else in their ministry.

Functioning members may be in two situations:

(a) Those who are feeling **fulfilled** in their ministry. They are diligent, active and effective in serving the church. Be encouraged, for 'great is your reward.'

(b) Those who are feeling **frustrated** in their ministry, maybe because of discouragement, tiredness or not feeling valued. Be encouraged, God sees you! Ministry will not be problem-free but the rewards are great. Discern the source of your frustration and try to deal with it. Ask for help from others whom you respect.

Don't neglect your gift. Stir it up. Use it for the benefit of others and the glory of God. The ball is in your court. What are you going to do about it? It's up to you.

First Things First

Jesus tells us to seek **first** the kingdom of God and all the other necessities of life will be added to us (Matthew 6:33). When we put God's kingdom as our first priority, we will know the blessing of God in every area of our lives.

Life is busy and has many pressures – many things to worry about. We all have family concerns and pressures, work or career pressures, study pressures if you're at school or university and financial pressures in addition to the stress and pressure created by our fast-paced society and the other problems in the world around us. There's plenty to worry about, yet Jesus tells us not to worry (Matthew 6:25–34). Put God first and all these other things will take care of themselves.

The issue is 'What's first?' It's a matter of priority, focus and importance. All these things have to be dealt with and are part of life, but if we focus first on them, we'll be consumed with worry and anxiety. When we focus first on the kingdom of God and on living for Him, then we will have God's help in handling all these other things.

God wants us to give Him the 'first things' in our lives:

• The first day of the week (the 'Lord's Day').

- The first part of each day.
- The first ten percent of all our income.
- The first part of our time, gifts and abilities for extending the kingdom.

The Old Testament book of Haggai gives us an example of what happens when God's people neglect God's house and put their own houses first. The Israelites had returned from captivity and had begun rebuilding the temple in Jerusalem, but because of opposition, they only completed the foundation. Work on God's house then stopped. They were under a curse and they were struggling in every area of life. Sixteen years later, God raised up the prophets Zechariah and Haggai to preach. The Jews were more to blame for the situation than any enemies they may have had and prophets tried to arouse them from their lethargy.

Haggai showed the people the consequences of disobedience (Haggai 1:6, 11; 2:16–17) and the blessings of obedience (Haggai 2:7–9, 19). He told them that when they gave priority to God and His house, they would be blessed rather than cursed. He told the people to *'Give careful thought to their ways'* (Haggai 1:5, 7; 2:15, 18) and he told the leaders and the people to be strong and finish the work of God's house (Haggai 2:4).

The people responded to the prophet and finished building the temple. From the very day that they put God's house first, God's blessing was released into their lives (Haggai 2:18–19).

The message is still the same today: If we put God's house first, He will bless our house. Put first things first. Jesus is building His house, which is His church. God wants all of us working with Jesus as He builds His church. We are God's fellow-workers and we are co-laboring with Him (1 Corinthians 3:9).

Building God's House

There are seven basic things that every Christian can do to see the church realize its full potential in God as we make this important **Ministry Shift**.

1. **Pray** (1 Timothy 2:1). We have already seen that prayer is to be the number one priority in the Church. Jesus said His Father's house is to be a 'House of prayer for all nations'. Prayer makes the difference between victory and defeat (Exodus 17:8–13). Paul constantly asked for prayer – for open doors and for God's blessing. Prayer brings God's blessing and power. It is the key to breakthrough. Pray for your church and its leadership on a daily basis.

2. **Worship** (John 4:20–24). Put God first by loving Him with all your heart, soul, mind and strength. Make praise, worship and thanksgiving a lifestyle. Don't neglect the corporate gathering of believers (Hebrews 10:25). Give God the first day of the week and gather with God's people for prayer, worship, teaching and direction. Come with faith and expectation and be responsive to what God is doing.

3. **Love** (1 Peter 4:8–9; John 15:12). Treat others the way you want to be treated. Encourage people, listen, forgive and offer help. Love in word and action. Put others first. Be friendly and welcome new people. Be hospitable and open your heart and your home to people. We live in a fragmented society looking for genuine love. Reach out and touch someone today.

4. **Protect the unity** (Ephesians 4:3). United we stand, divided we fall. Unity brings the blessing of God. Strife, discord, division and conflict destroy the Church. Guard the unity of your church. Watch for gossip, rumors and discord. We all have the ministry of reconciliation. Be a peacemaker.

5. **Serve** (1 Peter 4:10; Romans 12:6–8). Join the team. You have a gift, a place and a job to do. Be a contributor, not a spectator.

6. **Give** (Malachi 3:8–12). Get in on God's financial program. Bring your 'first fruits' or the 'tithe' (ten percent) of all your income into God's house, which is the local church where you are fed and cared for

(Proverbs 3:9–10). Be generous in your offerings. You will reap in proportion to your sowing.

7. **Reach out** (Matthew 28:18–20; 1 Timothy 2:1–7). Get actively involved in outreach, missions and evangelism. We exist for mission. Have an outward focus. Be a witness. Be 'salt and light'. Be a friend to the unchurched and pray for their salvation. Invite them to church. Do the work of an evangelist.

These seven simple things are like **power tools** that build the house of God. Every Christian can do them and when they do, there is blessing, fruitfulness, growth, fulfillment and joy for the Church and everyone in it. Building takes commitment, hard work, discipline, faithfulness and determination, but it's worth it when we're doing it for God.

I Have a Dream

I have a dream of churches all across the land filled with people using their gifts for the glory of God. Ordinary people touching other people for God. Action people, equipped, fervent and mobilized in ministry with a mission in every heart. People who refuse to let life pass them by and who have made a decision to make their life count for God. People of destiny who make a difference in the world around them. You can be one of them. Let's help the Church to be transformed by making a **Ministry Shift**.

Notes

1. The major points in this section about God's Team have been adapted from John Maxwell's *Lay Ministry* training kit, available from INJOY.

2. See Ephesians 4:11–16, Romans 12:1–2, 3–8 and 1 Corinthians 12–14.

3. Peter Wagner's book *Your Spiritual Gifts Can Help Your Church Grow* is an excellent resource on the subject of spiritual gifts (Ventura, California: Regal Books, 1994).

4. **Willow Creek Community Church** has prepared an excellent resource called *Network* that is designed to help believers discover, develop and use their spiritual gifts.

5. In the *Lay Ministry* training kit mentioned above, John Maxwell has a video using the analogy of the church as a football team. The following points have been adapted from this video.

6. Larry Stockstill gives some recommendations on how to do this in his book *The Cell Church*.

Personal Action Plan

Here are some ideas to help you make a personal **Ministry Shift**:

1. Find out what areas of ministry in your church need volunteer help and make yourself available.
2. Take a 'spiritual gift' questionnaire and/or personality test and discover your unique God-given abilities.
3. Ask one of the church leaders or a close friend to give you some feedback as to what they see are your strengths and future ministry potential.
4. Think about what you enjoy doing, or what areas of ministry interest you. Talk to someone who is active in these areas and learn all you can about this area of ministry.
5. Cultivate a servant attitude every day. Make it your aim to help every person that you come in contact with.

Church Action Plan

Here are some ideas to help your church make a **Ministry Shift**:

1. Give a series of sermons on spiritual gifts and the importance of serving.
2. Gather a list of ministry opportunities in the church and have a sign up for those who'd like to get involved.
3. Implement a gift analysis program to help people in your congregation determine their spiritual gifts.
4. Honor and profile your volunteers in every area of ministry, especially those who serve behind the scenes. Write them letters of thanks, have a servant spotlight in a Sunday meeting or put on a special dinner for them.

SHIFT 6

A Worldview Shift from a church mentality to a kingdom mentality

'My prayer is . . . that all of them may be one, Father, just as you are in me and I am in you. May they also be in us so that the world may believe that you have sent me.'

(John 17:20–21)

Becoming a United Community

A Worldview Shift

The next shift is a **Worldview Shift** that requires us to shift from having a narrow, local church focus to having a much broader kingdom mentality.

In Mark 9:38–40, we have an interesting story involving Jesus' disciples. While travelling along ministering in various villages, they observed someone else ministering. They said,

> *'Jesus, we saw someone who is **not one of us** casting out demons in your name. Should we tell them to stop?'*

Notice how their reaction revealed an attitude of pride and exclusiveness that Jesus had to rebuke them for.

This story reveals some common attitudes that can easily become part of our way of thinking concerning other churches and ministries. Like the disciples, we need to change our thinking patterns in order to adopt a **kingdom mentality**. We need to shift our focus so that we do not merely concentrate our attention on our own local church or ministry, but begin to see what God is doing through the wider Church and the Body of Christ.

Other ministries need to be valued and respected, as long as they are building the kingdom of God. Those who are not working against us are actually working for us.

Here are some excellent attitudes that we need to embrace.

Be humble not proud

No ministry or local church has it all. No one has a corner on the truth and no one has arrived. No one ministry or local church is God's only instrument or the one true Church. We are all parts of the Body of Christ, which is made up of every

Christian and every church that declares Jesus Christ as Lord. Each one of us is special and unique, but we also need to value the uniqueness of others.

Humility demands that we have a sober or balanced view of ourselves. We must not think of ourselves more highly than we should (Romans 12:3). Each individual ministry or church is only a **part** of what God is doing. We all need each other. The Great Commission is too big for any one of us to fulfill. We need all churches and all Christian ministries working together to achieve God's purposes.

Praise God for the huge variety and diversity of ministries He is using today. We can learn from each one of them. God is delighted when we embrace a teachable attitude that refuses to become comfortable but seeks to keep learning and growing.

The book of Proverbs tells us that a mark of wisdom and maturity is a willingness to listen and learn from others (Proverbs 9:9; 12:15).

God hates pride (Proverbs 6:16–17; James 4:6–7). Pride goes before a fall and any ministry or local church that thinks too highly of itself sets itself up for self-destruction. Let's clothe ourselves with an attitude of humility.

Be inclusive, not exclusive

God desires us to seek to include others rather than exclude them. Christian love is expressed by an open, warm, embracing attitude toward other ministries and churches. We should look for common ground and not focus only on our differences (Philippians 1:15–18).

The apostle Paul's aim in each new relationship was to win everyone, and he did this by finding points of agreement and then seeking to influence people towards Christ and further maturity (1 Corinthians 9:19–23).

God wants us **connected** to others, not isolated from them. Cross-pollination leads to growth and improvement. We should seek to maintain balance and avoid the extremes that often occur through isolation.

God values diversity, not uniformity and so should we. In the Old Testament, there was only one nation of Israel, but it was made up of twelve different tribes, which were further made up of many different households and families. So it is in the Church today. There are many different denominations, associations, networks and groups of churches and ministries. Each is unique and has its own distinctives, but we are all a part of the one true Church. We are all brothers and sisters in Christ.

We must avoid prejudice against other churches and ministries and watch out that we don't develop stereotypes of other ministries based on gossip and hearsay, rather than personal experience.

Carnality and immaturity are evidenced by comparing one ministry against another and by forming little fan clubs around Christian superstars. Paul had to address these attitudes in the church at Corinth, because they were divided over various popular ministries of that time – Apollos, Peter and Paul (1 Corinthians 3:1–9). Paul had to show them that each ministry has its place and that God used them all to build His kingdom. Ultimately, the glory goes to God, who makes all things grow.

Many people ask, 'What about ministries or churches that don't believe what we believe?' Obviously, our fellowship is to be based on the fundamentals of the faith. However, we need to know the difference between non-negotiables (the absolutes of Scripture) and non-essentials (personal convictions and preferences). We should not judge one another on issues of conscience, preference or personal opinion (Romans 14:1–13).

God has called us to build bridges, not walls. The world will know we are Christians by our love for one another, and that is demonstrated by how we relate to other churches and Christian ministries.

Any ministry or local church that isolates itself from others becomes exclusive and eventually degenerates. Let's open up our hearts and reach out to others.

Discern, don't judge

I'm amazed and saddened at the amount of literature that is being produced today by Christians that is aimed at judging other churches or ministries and even going to the extreme of labeling them 'demonic' or 'of the devil.'[1]

The Bible does tell us to test all things and to hold on to the good and let the bad go (1 Thessalonians 5:21–22). 1 John 4:1–3 also tells us to test the spirits and to not believe everything we hear. We should test churches and ministries by what they say about Jesus – who He is and what He has done. We should, however, place final judgement on nothing before its time (1 Corinthians 4:5; James 4:10–12). God is the true judge, and each person will stand before Him (not us) and give account for all they have done.

Christian love requires us to avoid a critical attitude that is quick to pull down and point out flaws in other people and their ministries (Matthew 7:1–5). Instead of judging, Jesus tells us to examine the fruit or results of a person or ministry.

Derek Prince recommends five key things that we should look for when discerning whether any church, ministry or so-called 'move of God' is genuine or not.[2] Here they are:

1. The fruit of repentance. Are people turning from sin to God?

2. Respect for the Scriptures. Is God's Word being respected, valued and taught?

3. Exaltation of Jesus. Is Jesus being lifted up and magnified?

4. Love for other Christians. Is there a growing love for other believers?

5. Loving concern for the unreached. Is there a focus on reaching people for Christ?

A tree is known by its fruit. We may not always recognize or understand how the Spirit moves, but we can know the evidence of the Spirit's work. Is the **fruit** something that looks like the Holy Spirit?

Derek Prince goes on to say,

'If a significant number of Christians in the current move (or church or ministry) successfully passes all, or most, of the five tests, then it is safe to conclude that this is, essentially, a move of God. However, this does not mean that everyone or everything in it is faultless. God has no faultless people to work with, but it is amazing what He can do with those totally surrendered to Him, though weak and fallible.'

(Please also note that the devil does not want these five things to happen!)

We see this gracious attitude portrayed so beautifully in the advice that Gamaliel gave to the Pharisees when they were considering persecuting the early Church. In Acts 5:33–39, he tells them that, if this ministry is not of God, it will die down and come to nothing. However, if it is of God, they should leave it alone lest they be seen as fighting against God.

We would be wise to take his advice today as we observe other ministries and churches.

Love, don't hate

God has commanded us to love other Christians who also love Jesus!

We have been called to bless, not curse. We are to pray for God's blessing on other churches and ministries. We are to rejoice when they grow and sorrow when they struggle.

One of my good friends, Peter McHugh, who pastors a large church in our city, says, 'If the church across town is growing then my church is growing.' What a wonderful attitude to adopt. We are working together for the benefit of God's kingdom. We are not in opposition or competition with each other.

God is actually angry when we fight and hurt each other. When my two boys fight, my first concern is not to determine who was right or wrong, but that they stop fighting. Yes, the issues are important and they need to be sorted out, but my major goal is to stop them fighting and see them loving and respecting each other as brothers. I believe this is the Father's heart as He looks at the Church today. I hear Him saying, 'Stop fighting, you're brothers and sisters in Christ!'

Jesus said,

> *'By this will all people know you are my disciples ... by your love for one another.'*   (John 13:35)

God's will is that we come to the *'unity of the Spirit'* (Ephesians 4:3) and eventually to a *'unity of the faith'* (Ephesians 4:13).

God's Sheep

Each Christian is described as one of God's 'sheep', who He personally loves and cares for. He delegates this responsibility of care to leaders in the church, or shepherds who represent Him on earth.

Notice Jesus' last concern as He spoke to Peter before He ascended to heaven. Three times He said to Peter, 'Feed my sheep' (John 21:15–17). He wanted Peter, as a prominent leader in the early Church, to have the heart of a shepherd and to care for each individual.

Each local church is similar to a sheepfold, where a group of God's sheep are being cared for and led by one of God's 'under-shepherds'. Church leaders must recognize that each Christian is ultimately God's sheep. Leaders are to care for, feed and provide guidance to each person entrusted to them by God.

From time to time, God moves His sheep from fold to fold. Often, it's through relocation or a job transfer. Other times, it's because a new phase of growth is needed that requires a new environment. I heard one pastor of a growing church say, 'We don't steal sheep, we just grow grass.' This humorous statement has a lot of truth to it. Sheep that aren't getting fed or who aren't being cared for will move on to greener pastures.

Individual Christians that move to another local church need to ensure that they leave with a proper attitude and that they resolve any outstanding issues, if at all possible. Church-hopping is definitely not God's plan. Moving to a new church needs a lot of prayer and appropriate counsel.

When people leave our local church and join another church, we must continue to love them and treat them as brothers or sisters in Christ.

That They May Be One

God is building His Church, and His Church is an extension of the kingdom of God in every locality. It is not one particular denomination or nationalistic group. It is His people, out of every nation and cultural background. There are all kinds of different churches to reach all kinds of different people. As the true Church of Jesus Christ turns from competitiveness to co-operation, we will see the task of reaching our cities accomplished much more quickly.

A **kingdom mentality** sees the Church in the world as a body comprised of many local churches, all working together for God's purposes. It is a day of partnership and networking, based on relationship, not on the particular label a specific church or ministry may have.[3]

One of the most exciting events I attended this year was a gathering of senior leaders, from congregations of over five hundred people, from around Australia and New Zealand. There were about seventy-five people who attended this three-day conference of interaction and sharing.

The atmosphere was fantastic. Leaders came with a hunger and a desire to learn from one another and to build closer relationships with each other. The most amazing thing was the diversity of denominational background. There were Anglicans, Baptists, Churches of Christ, Pentecostals and a variety of other churches.

This kind of gathering is becoming normal and a part of everyday Christianity in our time. This is not some ecumenical movement being externally forced upon us, but rather an inner working of the Holy Spirit to bring God's people together in unity.

Just look at the number of things that are happening to bring the Church together:

1. **Pastor's prayer summits** – pastors and leaders are going away for four-day retreats with no agenda but to seek God and pray together.

2. **City-wide worship events** – churches are gathering together *en masse* to worship Jesus Christ as Lord.

3. **Promise Keepers** – men from all different churches are gathering together to inspire one another to true Christian manhood.

4. **Conferences and seminars** – people from all different churches are gathering together to learn from others.

5. **Global marches** – Christians are taking to the streets to show the world the love and joy of Christ.

6. **Prayer events** – times of united prayer are occurring where Christians are joining together during a defined period of time to focus on specific prayer requests.

7. **Missions enterprises** – churches are networking together to reach the unreached peopled groups of the world with the gospel.

It's a new day! God is breaking down the walls. He is bringing His body, the Church, together as a mighty force in the earth. It will take the whole Church, taking the whole gospel to the whole world, to complete the Great Commission. The last prayer of Jesus was that we would all be one as He and the Father are one (John 17:20–21). That is one prayer that will be answered. Let's work together for its fulfillment in our time as we make this important **Worldview Shift**.

Notes

1. It is important to 'contend for the faith once delivered to the saints' and stand for truth. However, we must focus on the fundamentals of Scripture and the essential doctrines of the Christian faith, not on minor controversial issues. We should also do everything in the spirit of Christ, which requires a loving and sensitive approach when speaking about other Christian ministries.

2. This is from a booklet by Derek Prince entitled *Uproar in the Church* (Derek Prince Ministries).

3. For an interesting book on what God is doing in the Church today, read *The New Apostolic Churches* by Peter Wagner (Ventura, California: Regal, 1998).

Personal Action Plan

Here are some ideas to help you make a personal **Worldview Shift**:

1. Visit other churches, conferences or events occasionally and develop an appreciation for the wider Church of Jesus Christ.

2. Fellowship with Christians from other churches.

3. Love and support your own local church, but avoid developing an attitude of superiority.

4. Refuse to listen to any gossip or rumors about another church or ministry without speaking directly to the appropriate person.

5. Pray for other churches and ministries in your city.

6. Attend any city-wide combined prayer meetings or worship events.

Church Action Plan

Here are some ideas to help your church make a **Worldview Shift**:

1. Begin to reach out to pastors of different churches in your city or local area. Invite them around for a meal in your home. Be interested in other people's ministry, not just your own.
2. Attend any combined pastors' events.
3. Join in with, and possibly organize, a combined churches prayer meeting or worship event.
4. When other churches or ministries are doing well, rejoice and congratulate them.
5. When other churches or ministries are struggling, pray for them and reach out to support them.
6. Refuse to listen to any gossip or rumors about another church or ministry without speaking directly to the appropriate person.
7. Attend conferences or events hosted by other churches or ministries. Be open and learn all you can. Glean principles for your own ministry while avoiding mere imitation of other people's methods.
8. Invite a variety of visiting ministries to your church to supplement your own local ministry.
9. Read books by authors who see things differently to you. Seek to understand their perspective.
10. Be firm in your own convictions but don't judge others.

SHIFT 7

A Generation Shift
from the older to younger

*'Now also when I am old and grey-headed, O God,
do not forsake me, until I declare Your strength
to this generation, Your power to everyone
who is to come.'*
(Psalm 71:18, NKJV)

Passing the Baton

Generation Next

Joshua was a fantastic leader. He took the baton from his mentor, Moses, then he ran an incredible race, serving his own generation by helping them take possession of the entire Promised Land. He motivated his own generation to serve God all the days of his life, and the lives of the other leaders who outlived him. But Joshua failed to do one important task. He failed to pass the baton on to the next generation. He did not train a successor. After Joshua died, there arose another generation, who did not know the Lord and they drifted from God's purposes for many years (Joshua 24:31; Judges 2:7–11).

There is no success without a successor. In fact, Christianity is always one generation away from extinction. We must have a **generation perspective**.

The Church today faces some major challenges. One of them is the need to pass on the purposes of God to the next generation. The largest churches that existed in America twenty years ago are either no longer in existence or have declined. Here in my home country, many Australian churches are dying or decreasing in numbers. The ones that are growing are realizing the need to reach the next generation with the gospel – our children and our young people.

The last **Strategic Shift** the Church must make is a **Generation Shift** from the older to the younger. This is not an issue of age (every older person was once a young person and every young person will one day be an older person!). It is a matter of building for the future.

God's Plan for the Generations

The dictionary tells us that a generation is a group of people of like nature either by age or distinguishing characteristics (such as 'evil' or 'righteous').

In Isaiah 41:4, the prophet says that God has *'called the generations from the beginning.'* God is carrying out His purposes through generations of the righteous. We each need to have a sense of destiny in our heart and we must see ourselves as part of the unfolding plan of God throughout the ages of time, not as a separate entity without a past or a future. A study of the entire Bible reveals that each generation has certain responsibilities before God.[1]

1. To discern and accomplish the will of God for their generation

Every generation is responsible to fulfill God's will for their time in history. We each have a race to run and a role to play in carrying out God's purposes. We must give ourselves to discovering and passionately pursuing our unique destiny.

> *'For when David had served God's purpose in his own generation, he fell asleep; he was buried with his fathers and his body decayed.'* (Acts 13:36)

> *'Now also when I am old and grey-headed, O God, do not forsake me, until I declare Your strength to this generation, your power to everyone who is to come.'* (Psalm 71:18)

2. To rebuild the foundations from past generations

Every generation is responsible to reach back and receive an inheritance from those who have gone before. We did not begin this race. We simply carry it on. We are to build on the truths and experiences of those who have gone before. Godly people have left us a legacy which we are to build upon. We must discover and value our roots and our heritage.

> *'Those from among you shall build the old waste places; you shall raise up the foundations of many generations; and you shall be called the Repairer of the Breach, the Restorer of Streets to Dwell In.'* (Isaiah 58:12, NKJV)

> *'And they shall rebuild the old ruins, they shall raise up the former desolations, and they shall repair the ruined cities, the desolations of many generations.'* (Isaiah 61:4, NKJV)

3. To pass on truth to the next generation and guide them into a personal experience with God

Each generation is responsible to pass the baton of God's purposes on to the next generation. God requires us to leave a heritage and an inheritance for those who follow after us.

As Steve Green sings in the powerful song, *Find us Faithful*,

'May the footprints that we leave, cause them to believe and may all who come behind us find us faithful.'

'Now also when I am old and grey-headed, O God, do not forsake me, until I declare Your strength to this generation, your power to everyone who is to come.'
(Psalm 71:18, NKJV)

'We will not hide them from their children, telling to the generation to come the praises of the Lord, and His strength and His wonderful works that He has done.'
(Psalm 78:4, NKJV)

Satan's Plot for the Generations [2]

Satan also has a plan for the generations that we need to be aware of as we make this **Generation Shift**. The devil endeavors to deceive and destroy each generation and his focus is always on the young. He also wants to put conflict between parents and children, thereby alienating each generation from the previous one. There has been enmity and conflict between Satan's offspring and the woman's, ever since the fall of Adam and Eve (Genesis 3:15).

The apostle Peter tells us that the devil is like a roaring lion, seeking whom he can devour (1 Peter 5:8–9). In Revelation 12, the apostle John describes his vision of a great dragon, symbolizing the devil. He is incredibly angry, because he knows that he has only a short time. The dragon is enraged with the woman, symbolic of the Church, and he goes to make war with her offspring, who keep the commandments of God and have the testimony of Jesus Christ. Satan hates the Church and the generation of the righteous. He is seeking to deceive the whole world.

Satan wants to destroy each new generation of young people because they have the potential to subdue him. He uses things such as suicide, the occult, drug and alcohol abuse, violence, Satanism and immorality. He comes to steal (rob, take away), kill (damage, scar, ruin potential) and ultimately to destroy their lives (John 10:10).

Wendell Smith, in his *Dragon Slayer* seminars, presents five challenges that each young person faces today. Here is a brief summary of these *Battlezones of Youth Culture*:

1. Rebellion – the Search for Security

Satan takes advantage of young people's reaction to human authority and, out of their hurt and hatred, stirs up a spirit of rebellion against the authority of God.

Satan is the original rebel. When young people rebel, they co-operate with the spirit of Satan (Ephesians 2:1–3). In the last days, we are told that people will be disobedient to parents (2 Timothy 3:2). In encouraging young people to rebel against authority, the enemy robs them of God's blessing and the potential of character development. Rebellion destroys young people and the family (1 Samuel 15:23).

God's answer to rebellion is yielded control to authority. God wants young people who will radically dedicate their lives to His loving Lordship and obediently submit to the authority of His Word, His Spirit and His representatives.

God has put authorities over our life to develop character in us and to provide covering and protection. God-ordained authorities include parents (Ephesians 6:1), the government (1 Peter 2:13–17; Romans 13:1–7), teachers or employers (Colossians 3:22) and church leaders (Hebrews 13:17).

We must model obedience to our children and teach them the principles of God's Word. Obeying God means obeying His representatives. Authority is the tool in God's hand that He uses to mature us.

Young people need clear boundaries to live within, and discipline when they cross over them. Teenagers need both privileges and responsibilities. All of this needs to be in the context of a loving relationship. Josh McDowell says, 'Rules without a relationship equals rebellion.'

2. Immorality – the Search for Affection

Looking for attention, affection and meaningful relationships, young people often fall into Satan's trap of deceitful desires and sexual immorality. In the last days, we are told that people will be without self-control and lovers of pleasure (2 Timothy 3:3–4).

Satan's plan is to destroy the family and rob children of a healthy environment. He does this through things such as conflict, abuse, divorce and busyness. Young people with a shortage of love, approval, acceptance and affection, will find them somehow. Many yield to the temptation of sexual involvement outside of marriage – because of curiosity, heightened sexual desires, peer pressure and the need for affection and belonging.

The results may be unwanted pregnancy, abortion, disease, loss of virginity, guilt, low self-esteem, negative feelings about sex, difficulty in breaking off a bad relationship, performance orientation, a wounded soul and broken fellowship with God. Later, these can result in a difficult courtship, communication breakdown in marriage, comparison of past sexual partners and disillusionment with relationships or marriage.

Sexual immorality affects you more than any other sin. Ask Samson or David. Paul tells us that when a person sins sexually, they sin against their own body (1 Corinthians 6:18).

Youth culture has a strong sexual orientation, and we live in a society that has gone sex-mad. It is estimated that ninety-four percent of sexual encounters portrayed on television and in the movies are between people who are not married.

Satan has taken what God created to be a lifelong, beautiful relationship between two people and perverted it. There is great pressure on young people to conform to the world.

The Bible clearly tells us that those who live immoral lifestyles will not inherit the kingdom of God (1 Corinthians 6:9–11). We reap what we sow (Galatians 6:7–8). Sexual sin is a work of the sinful nature (Galatians 5:13–21) and, if not repented of, can cause people to forfeit entrance into the kingdom of God.

God's intention is that the family provides an environment of love, approval, acceptance and affection. Sexual desires are to be controlled before marriage. Once a young person reaches maturity, they then enter marriage, free of hurts and scars, to begin a family of their own.

God's answer to immorality and the search for affection is love expressed through selfless giving. Those who are truly freed from the bondage of sin and rebellion can experience the covenant relationships and pure affection of the Body of Christ and learn to treat each another in love as brothers and sisters.

Young people need to develop healthy brother-sister relationships where wholesome friendships can be built. They need to understand God's will for their life, the various levels of friendship, and the appropriate age and behavior for each.

Young people need to be taught the value of virginity and purity and the honor of marriage as God intended it to be (Hebrews 13:4). Those involved in a romantic relationship need to understand the dangers, and set goals and guidelines together to ensure that they act in a way which is pleasing to God and without defrauding each other. There needs to be a balance of time, words and actions. A serious romantic relationship, involving physical contact without any intention of marriage, is an abuse of one another's emotions. Young people should be on guard against temptation and wrong or premature desires (1 Thessalonians 4:1–8; 1 Timothy 5:1–2; 1 Peter 1:22).

3. Sorcery – the Search for the Supernatural

There is, in the heart of every young person, a hunger for spiritual reality and a desire to experience the world of the supernatural. Drugs and alcohol are artificial attempts to find that world and they open the soul to Satanic influence. In the last days, we know that people will have a form of godliness, but deny its power (2 Timothy 3:5).

Sorcery comes from the Greek word *pharmakeia* from which we get the word 'pharmacy'. It refers to magic, drugs and spells. It is a work of the sinful nature (Galatians 5:19–21) and it is subject to eternal judgement (Revelation 9:21; 21:8; Acts 8:9–25; 13:6–12).

Alcohol abuse is rampant. Drunkenness often leads to crime, violence and an escalating road toll. What a tragic effect drinking has on our families and community. Other drugs are also very accessible to the average teenager at high school or from friends. Peer pressure and boredom cause many young people to turn to drugs. Standing out from the crowd as different is one of the hardest things for a teenager to do.

There is also an increasing involvement of young people in the occult and Satanism as they look to the supernatural out of curiosity.

God's answer to sorcery and the search for the supernatural is the power of the Holy Spirit and a demonstration of faith. When a young believer experiences the supernatural manifestation of the Holy Spirit's power, it makes all other counterfeits cheap and temporal and introduces them to a new realm of faith.

God's kingdom is not just words but power (1 Corinthians 4:20; 2:4–5; Acts 1:8). Young people need to see and experience God's power in their lives. God's power moves supernaturally in our spirit, soul and body. The Spirit-filled believer does not need the 'power' of drugs and alcohol to cope with the realities of life.

4. Fantasy – the Search for Reality

Today's hyper-interest in mythology and science fiction is a prophetic fulfillment of the Scriptures and a subtle but powerful distraction to the minds of the younger generation. In the last days, many will turn aside to fables (2 Timothy 4:4).

Many young people live in a world of fantasy and imagination. Television, videos, computer games, internet surfing, role playing games, music and virtual reality take up hours of leisure time providing an escape from the real world. Life seems boring. Too much fantasy damages young people and destroys the family.

God's answer to fantasy is truth or ultimate reality. The Lord is raising up a generation of young men and women whose minds have been renewed by the reality and truth of His Word and whose lifestyles reflect the superior principles of the Holy Scriptures (John 8:32).

Young people need to be taught to have a love for the Bible and be equipped to not only read it, but to study and apply it to their daily lives. God's Word has the answers to all of the questions and problems that we face. Youth need to learn how to face the realities of life and live with joy and hope without having to escape through fantasy. We must help them develop personal convictions so that they can stand against peer pressure like Daniel.

God does not want us to build our lives on fantasy, fables, myths and the philosophies of men (1 Timothy 4:6–7; 2 Timothy 4:2–4; 2 Thessalonians 2:9–17.) Life can be enjoyable and fun, but we must build on the basics of routine, discipline, work and quality relationships.

5. Idolatry – the Search for a God

Satan uses dynamic and beautiful music to arouse desire in young people that manifests itself in the idolatrous worship of people or things, deceiving young people into actually worshipping Satan. In the last days, people will be lovers of pleasure more than lovers of God (2 Timothy 3:4).

We live in a world of hero worship. People are on a search for a god or someone to worship and to follow after. Music is not just entertainment. Music and its artists are worshipped today by young people.

Music is the most important aspect of youth culture. It is a message bearer, an identity former, an emotional drug, a passive escape and a medium for transcendent experience. It is representative of the values of youth culture and it is a powerful medium for their message. Music presents all of the battlezones of youth culture on a continual basis – **rebellion** (anger, violence), **immorality** (rock music's number one message), **sorcery** (singers use and promote drugs, alcohol and the occult), **fantasy** (escapism) and **idolatry**.

God's answer to idolatry and the search for a god is worship and expressing our love for Him. God is seeking a generation to worship Him. Only when we worship Him in Spirit and truth can we come to know what it means to love the Lord our God with all our heart, soul, mind and strength (Philippians 3:3; John 4:20–24; Luke 24:50–53).

In Matthew 4:10, Jesus said to the devil,

'Away with you, Satan! For it is written, "You shall worship the Lord your God, and Him only you shall serve."'

Young people need to know God's heart and understand God's incredible love for them. He wants to give us life and the very best. He wants to keep us from Satan's schemes. He has a purpose, a plan and a destiny for each of us. In response, young people need to dedicate their entire lives to God, endeavoring to live in a way that will bring glory to Him. Music can be used as a tool to express our love to God in dynamic worship and praise. We should love God above all else. Don't allow love for anything else to draw your affections away from God.

People of Destiny

Wendell Smith goes on to say,

'There is a spiritual war on and thousands of young people are becoming its victims. There's no neutral ground. Overcome or be overcome. Every young person is a target. However, God is raising up an army of young warriors who, despite the overwhelming odds, will overcome the enemy through the power of the Holy Spirit. These young men and women will have a powerful influence on today's youth culture as they fulfill God's purpose for this generation.'

In recognizing the battlezones youth are facing today, we cannot afford to simply deny, avoid or reject this new youth culture. We must seek to understand the world of our young people and impart dynamic principles from God's Word that will enable them to be overcomers.

Our goal must be to establish a sense of purpose and destiny in each young person's heart that will motivate them to seek to discover and fulfill God's purpose for their life. Each young person is born to win, to overcome and to be a champion. God is the ultimate victor, and He wants us to partake of His power and victory even in the face of overwhelming odds. Joshua did it at Jericho. Gideon did it. David defeated Goliath, and we can help young people defeat the giants of our day.

God can give each young person the strength to overcome every attack of the enemy and preserve them for His purposes. Wendell Smith says,

> 'Young people ruled by their own sins and weaknesses become incompetent or poor citizens in their society, and contribute to the reproach and moral decay of a nation. Young people who conquer sin and temptation tend to become leaders in their society and bring stability and honor to their nation.'

Youth Culture

Are today's youth different to any other generation? Yes! We live in an era of unprecedented social change and technological explosion. There is a crumbling of old institutions and values. The social lifestyles of men, women and families are changing rapidly. In the midst of this tremendous change a new culture has emerged.

Youth culture is an entirely modern phenomenon that has swept the world in an incredibly short period of time. It's not a culture based on a certain nationality or people group, but on a specific age group – with their own music, clothes and way of life. Youth, as a separate grouping, had little existence until recent times. Satan is using youth culture as an orchestrated spiritual assault to steal an entire generation and eventually the whole world.

Satan's strategy is to capture the youth of the world by isolating them and gaining control of the carriers of youth culture – the arts, education and the electronic media. He is also using the youth culture to capture the wider adult world. The whole of society has taken on an adolescent tone or mentality. Youth culture is now being exported to the entire world. The majority of television programs, movies, videos, music, advertising and magazines are aimed at the youth.

Michael Keating says,

> 'One of the great tragedies of our day is the widening gap between teenagers and their parents. Young people live

in a world completely different to the world their parents lived in as teenagers. Pressure to use illegal drugs and alcohol can be almost impossible to stand up to. Group sex, satanic rituals and suicide are attractive options for far too many young people. Often teenagers feel that no one cares about them and that no one is listening.'[3]

There are five major challenges in reaching today's youth culture:

1. **The philosophy of humanism.** Most of today's educational systems have rejected the Judeo-Christian ethic. We live in a post-Christian society. Young people are growing up with no understanding of God, the Bible, the Ten Commandments or who Jesus is (other than a swear word). The basic tenets of humanism – atheism, evolution, amorality, autonomous man and a socialist worldview – form the foundation of most young people's worldview.

2. **The disintegration of the family unit.** We live in a world of broken homes, increasing divorce, rejection, rebellion and communication breakdown. The average teenager gets only two minutes of 'quality' time from their parent(s) each day. Young people are growing up with little or no love, acceptance or security.

3. **The prodigal son and the elder brother.** Unfortunately, some young people who are raised in the Church, and in Christian homes, backslide and leave the Father's house. However, God's heart reaches out to them and yearns for their repentance and reconciliation. So must we. When they do return, we must welcome them and not adopt an 'elder brother' attitude that despises or looks down on them.

4. **The increasing isolation and irrelevance of the Church.** The world is experiencing 'future shock' because of the rapid changes taking place. Christians and churches tend to become isolated and exist in a world of their own. If we build walls rather than bridges, we will have no hope of reaching those in need of the gospel.

5. **The restoration of ruined lives.** As young people are saved today, many of them come from a world of alcohol, drugs, sexual perversion and abuse. They need salvation, healing and deliverance from all that is in the past. Thankfully, the gospel is a new covenant of grace, where God can give us beauty for ashes. God's Spirit gives us the power to change and to be free from everything that holds us down.

Pass the Baton

As we reach out to the next generation, let's look together at those who have the main responsibility of preparing them to achieve their God-given destiny.

Parents

God requires parents to teach their children the ways of God, including His commands and principles for living. They are also responsible to guide their children into a personal relationship with God.

We all know the old song, 'Jesus loves the little children, all the children of the world.' Yes, it's true. He places them under the care and nurture of parents, who represent Him on earth.

In Ephesians 6:4, Paul says,

> '*Fathers* [or parents], *do not exasperate your children; instead, bring them up in the training and instruction of the Lord.*'

God holds parents responsible for the next generation. In the book of Deuteronomy, Moses tells the people over forty times that they must train the next generation in the ways of God (Deuteronomy 6:1–25).

Parents have these basic responsibilities:

- To love God with all their heart.

- To obey God's commandments.

- To impress God's commandments on their children through the daily events of life.

The word 'impress' means 'to teach diligently, consistently and with intensity, showing their importance'. The original Hebrew word gives us a word picture of sharpening a sword or arrow with a grindstone.

This was God's plan for Israel. As each child matured, he or she became responsible for the next generation and so on. God's purposes were to be communicated verbally and visually in the home, so that godliness and righteousness would pass from one generation to the next, so that they could be a blessing to the world. Each parent's primary responsibility was to see their children choose to love and serve God. God's plan is still the same today.

The family can't survive or be successful without our children – the next generation. As parents, we must train them through love and discipline, and, at the appropriate time, release them like arrows, finely honed to reach their God-given destiny. We all want to impact our world. It starts right at home, with our families.

The most impacting method of training our children is by our personal example. Children do what children see. They learn by watching our life, not just by hearing our words. Your life is your lesson. Who you are speaks louder than what you say.

Be a positive role model, a mirror, a reflection of what you're trying to teach. Paul told Timothy that his most powerful impact as a leader would be through being an example in his words, life, love, faith and purity (1 Timothy 4:12). Let's live a life worth imitating, so that our children want what we have.

Josh McDowell says, 'You can con a con, you can fool a fool, but you can't kid a kid.' [4] Be a hero to your kids by being someone they want to be like.

Ultimately, our children must make their own choices and they will be responsible for their own actions (Ezekiel 18:1–32). There will be prodigals. Even God the Father's first children, Adam and Eve, rebelled and ran from Him, despite receiving clear instructions and an explanation of the consequences of disobedience. However, we must do our very best to show our children the ways of God and bring them to know Him personally.

The Church

The church exists to support, not replace, the role of the parents in raising up the next generation for God. Part of each church's role is to help parents raise their children for God and to reach out to children who don't come from a Christian home. That's why every local church needs a dynamic ministry to children and young people.

The church must take its ministry to children and young people seriously. It is a very important ministry. There is a battle on for a generation.

Note Jesus' attitude to children. He said,

> '*Let the little children come to me,*'

> (Mark 10:14)

and

> '*Whoever welcomes a little child like this in my name welcomes me.*'   (Matthew 18:5)

Jesus loved and ministered to children. He even used children to teach adults.

Before ascending to His Father, Jesus said to Peter, 'Feed my sheep' **and** 'Feed my lambs'. Too often, churches emphasize feeding the sheep (adults) and ignore the lambs (children). The church's program is often geared to adults. If we want to make Jesus welcome in our churches, we need to make sure children feel accepted and appreciated. Churches must place a greater priority upon ministry to children and youth by giving them the very best resources.

Winning a child means saving a life. Children are tender and open to the gospel, a factor that often changes as they grow older. If we do not reach people in their youth, most of them will never be reached. Look at the following statistics: [5]

- Eighty-five percent of people come to Christ by the age of fifteen.

- Only one in 10,000 will come to Christ after the age of thirty.

- Only one in every 750,000 will come to Christ after the age of seventy-five.

The great evangelist, D.L. Moody, when asked how many

people were saved at a certain meeting, said 'Two and a half'. When asked if that meant two adults and a child, Moody replied, 'No.' It meant two children and one adult, he explained, because children had their entire lives ahead of them, but the lives of the adults were half over.

In a survey of the largest Bible seminary in America, it was found that sixty-five percent of the students accepted Christ before the age of thirteen. In another study of missionaries, seventy percent had been saved by the age of fourteen. Of that percentage the majority of them accepted Christ between five and nine years of age.[6]

The world's population is now over six billion. About half of the world's population are under the age of fourteen. 2.7 billion have not had an adequate presentation of the gospel, many of them children. Many children in our city don't go to church. There's a mission field right on our doorstep.

Satan does not wait until children become adults before seeking to destroy their lives. He begins in the womb – millions of babies are aborted each year. He then continues his attack, as he uses our culture to capture the minds and hearts of young people, often messing their lives up with drugs, sex and rebellion.

We must focus on children and young people as one of the church's greatest mission fields. No doubt, the largest churches of tomorrow will be the ones with the most dynamic children's ministries today because children and youth are the feeder systems of the church.

Church leaders

This **Generation Shift** is also leading to a change in the leadership of the church. There is no success without a successor, and wise older leaders are passing the baton on to the next generation, like Moses did to Joshua.

We need older men and women, who are in current leadership positions, to lift to a higher level by becoming spiritual fathers and mothers to a new generation of younger leaders.

Leadership transition is vital to the ongoing health and progress of each local church. As in a relay race, the passing of the baton is a strategic time that will make or break the overall result of the race. Waiting too long to pass the baton, or letting go too soon, can both spell disaster.

I am privileged to be leading a church that has had two successful leadership transitions, both resulting in the ongoing growth and health of the church. Our church was started in 1967 in a small shop front building, with a handful of people led by a wonderful man by the name of Richard Holland. Richard faithfully led the church for twenty years, growing it to a congregation of almost six hundred people through his contagious enthusiasm and love for God. He then turned the leadership over to my father, Kevin Conner, who led the church for the next seven years. In this time, the church grew to a congregation of almost fifteen hundred people, spurred on by my father's teaching and leadership gifts. Then in 1995, the leadership was passed on to me. By the grace of God, the church has continued to grow from strength to strength.

Richard is now over eighty years of age and my father is seventy-two years old. They are a source of constant encouragement to me as they continue on as part of our ministry team. They have not **retired**. They have **re-fired**, and continue to use their gifts to build both the local church and the wider Body of Christ.

Successful transition requires a good deal of personal security in the senior leader that enables them to let go properly. So often we find identity in the things we do – our ministry – rather than who we are, and this makes it difficult to pass on to others what we've worked so hard for. True spiritual fathers long to see their children rise and actually do better than they have.

For those of us who receive the inheritance that others have worked so hard for, we need to value and honor those who have gone before. True spiritual sons never get rid of fathers, but continue to respect the heritage they have. Sons become fathers and fathers become grandfathers as the family of God moves forward through the generations.

This leadership transition needs to happen at every level and in every area of ministry within the church. We must reach out to and seek to raise up, the next generation to take ownership and leadership within the local church.

Generational Waves

Passing the baton on to the next generation is not always easy. A generation gap that divides the young and the old is always a potential threat. Also, each new generation brings with it an whole new culture and different ways of doing things. This overlapping of the generations is like different waves that can crash into each other, causing much damage if not carefully managed.[7]

Let's first have a look at today's generations. We'll then have a look at some of the cultural changes taking place within the Church.

There are at least four different audiences, age groups, cultures and generations existing today. They each have a unique identity and a different way of seeing the world. They all coexist in our culture right now. Marketers and the media understand the differences between these generations and target them intentionally.

Sociologists categorize the current generations in a variety of ways. Here is a fairly common grouping of the generations with some general characteristics.

Builders

The Builders are people fifty years of age and older. They are also referred to as the 'Seniors' or the 'Survivors'. They were raised during the years of the Great Depression and World War II. They survived very harsh cultural and societal conditions, yet they brought about a very productive society. They experienced the greatest economic and industrial expansion in the history of civilization. Their formative years were the 1920s, 1930s and 1940s.

The people of this generation have been described as hard workers, savers, cautious, loyal, respectful, dependable and stable. They are somewhat intolerant at times, have skills and money, want to do something worthwhile with their life and have much to offer.

Areas of concern include financial security, health, adequate transportation, retirement options and survival, in a world where the ever-increasing pace of frenzied activity can be overwhelming.

Builder believers are usually very committed to the local church, support foreign missions, enjoy Bible study, are loyal to denominations, minister out of a sense of duty and like to worship in reverence. The Builders have been the funding base for most Christian organizations for decades. This generation has provided the predominant cultural mentality within the Church, with few exceptions.

This older generation needs appreciation, support, involvement, a sense of worth, pastoral care and meaningful contact with other generations. They have much to offer the younger generations, because of their wisdom and experience.

Baby Boomers

The Boomers are people from thirty-five to fifty years of age. They are the children of the Builders and are sometimes referred to as the 'Post-war babies'. They were raised during the Vietnam War, the Cultural Revolution of the 1960s, and in extreme affluence with opportunities unimaginable to their parents.

They are referred to as the 'Me Generation', the 60's Generation, yuppies (young urban professionals) or DINKs (Double Income, No Kids). Their formative years were the 1950s, 1960s and 1970s with strong musical influences from bands such as the Beatles and the Rolling Stones.

Boomers have been described as entertainment focused, faddish, intellectually lazy, somewhat optimistic, fitness conscious, media-orientated, independent, desirous of quality, tending to question authority, open to spiritual experience and devoted to rock culture. They are the most educated generation in history. They are the first generation reared on television and a world of new technology.

Boomer Christians are usually committed to relationships, want to belong, supportive of people rather than organizations, want to live their faith, want experiences with faith and tend to be tolerant of differences. Among other things, Boomers need a sense of meaning and purpose, stability and help with their family and career.

Boomers have burned out on popular culture, and attachment to traditional values and institutions is becoming more likely. Some are depressed and looking for answers. Others are looking for family values and want the Church to help them raise their kids. Some are burned out on the New Age and are looking for stability. Others are lonely and are looking for companionship. Still others have been disillusioned with life in general and are searching for meaning and purpose. The Boomer generation is at a crossroads, and the Church has a window of opportunity to reach them for Christ.

Western Christianity has been dominated by the Boomers parents' generation (Builders) that dislikes the culture of the 1960s. Boomers, despite their desire to return to a real spiritual experience, are unable to relate to a church culture dominated by their parents. It is a big leap for them to jump into traditional forms of worship and church that worked well before the 1960's. Though only one generation apart chronologically, these two generations are years apart culturally.[8]

Baby Busters

The Busters are people from twenty-five to thirty-five years of age. They are the children of the Boomers. They were born into a world of incredibly advanced technology, video games, computers, music and AIDS. Their formative years were the 1970s, 1980s and 1990s.

Busters have been described as skeptical, somewhat pessimistic, more conservative than their elders, not good at mingling with other groups, yet somewhat stable and able to work well together with people their own age. Busters are often environmentally conscious and interested in quality of life. Many are from broken homes and some have been neglected by parents who have been too busy and focused on their own careers and personal freedom to pay much attention to them.

Busters need close relationships and a strong sense of purpose. They can easily feel neglected and lonely. The Church can help this generation by offering vision, practical teaching, love and acceptance.[9]

Generation X

Generation X refers to young people from sixteen to twenty-five years of age.

This generation has been born into a world that is rapidly changing and moving forward, yet also declining at an incredible rate. They can tend to have low self-esteem resulting in them retreating from the world into small groups. Time will tell how this media-saturated generation will develop. Crimes are being committed at younger ages than ever before. On the other hand, the spiritual awareness of this young generation is very high. They can quickly lay hold of what God is doing and commit to it with a radical abandonment.

The Church can harness the energy of the young by offering love, acceptance, practical life-related teaching and a mission big enough for them to give their lives for.

Generation M

This is a title being given to the next yet-to-be-defined generation of children who have been born in the late 1990s. They will spend the majority of their lives in the new millennium, the year 2000 (Roman numeral 'M') and beyond, hence the name Generation M.

A Change in Church Culture

As each generational wave comes in, there is a resulting change in the culture of the Church. Although we must reject the sinful values of each new culture, we must distinguish these from the non-sinful customs, styles and preferences of each generation.

Truths and principles are eternal. They never change and neither does our message. However, our methods and emphases do and must change. Unless the Church continues to adapt and remain culturally relevant, it will lose a whole generation of young people.

Let's look at some obvious cultural changes taking place in the Church today, affected by the emergence of new generations.

Worship styles

There is a shift from old songs to new songs with a contemporary sound. Music is an integral part of our lives, yet it is an extremely divisive issue that separates generations, personality types and even family members. A person's musical tastes or preferences are usually determined by their background, age or culture.

James Dobson says that of all the subjects covered on his radio program, from abortion to pornography to whatever, the most controversial subject he's ever dealt with is music. His conclusion is that nothing can make people mad more quickly than the subject of music. Therefore, we should not be surprised when opinions of music differ in the Church.

The Bible clearly encourages us to use music to praise and worship God but does not define what style of music we should use or how loud or how fast it should be played.

In his book, *The Purpose Driven Church*, Rick Warren says that each church must decide on who they are trying to reach, identify their preferred musical style and then stick with it. More than anything else, the music played in your church will define who you are and who you are trying to reach.[10]

Rick Warren goes on to note that, today, the music of the 1960s and 1970s dominates our culture. Ninety-six percent of people listen to middle-of-the-road adult contemporary music. Most people under forty don't relate to any music before 1965. To them, a classic is an Elvis tune. In fact, only 2–8% of the population prefers classical music. They like bright, happy, cheerful music with a strong beat. For the first time in history, there exists a universal musical style that can be heard in every country of the world. It's called contemporary rock or pop music.

For the Church to be relevant to the younger generations, it must adapt its musical style of worship and seek to do things with greater excellence and quality. After all, God deserves our very best.

Dress styles

The younger generations tend to prefer informality. Formality is sometimes seen as being 'fake', while being casual is seen as more 'real'. Young people often say, 'Don't judge me for what I'm wearing. Appreciate me for who I am.'

When it comes to this area of dress, we must distinguish between biblical and cultural expectations. The biblical standards for dress are modesty and neatness. Everything else concerning dress style is either cultural or personal preference.

We all tend to judge people by their appearance, and this can lead to placing a greater emphasis on externals than on inward attitudes and character qualities of godliness. This was what Jesus rebuked the Pharisees for.

As Christians, we should avoid accepting people based on appearance. We should welcome everyone, and treat people with respect and warmth independent of their external appearance. They should not have to conform to be accepted. We should also be careful not to show partiality based on appearance (James 2:1–9).

This does not mean that there should be no standards within the Church or that excellence should not be pursued. However, we must be willing to accept diversity. Different generations dress differently and have different personal tastes. We must continue to uphold the biblical principles of modesty and excellence, while maintaining a love for people no matter what they look like.

Ministry style

Each new generation has different preferences when it comes to ministry style. The shift is from tradition to relevance, from distance to realness or vulnerability. The younger generation wants to know about our failures and fears. They are not just interested in titles, positions or qualifications. They are looking for someone to care about them and help them find meaning in their life. Relationship is stressed more as the glue that holds them together rather than structure and creeds. Humor and casualness are not seen as irreligious.

The younger generation is also more visual in their learning style, due to the tremendous increase of technology. Rather than sit and listen to a one-hour lecture, they prefer a sermon to include things such as drama, stories, illustrations, music or multi-media to enhance the message.

Note these other characteristics of the younger generations:

- They like to participate in what's happening.

- They tend to be non-institutional and are therefore low on denominational loyalty.

- They are more experience orientated.

- They are extremely pragmatic in their sermon tastes. Practical living is where it's at.

- They believe women need to be represented in leadership.

- They expect that the contribution of singles will be celebrated and accepted. For instance, over fifty percent of the adult population in America is now single.

- The increasing level of dysfunction among these generations needs to be faced. Sexual abuse and homosexuality are becoming more common. Recovery groups and skilled counseling is a must to deal sensitively with these very painful issues and with hurting people.

- They applaud innovation. Multiple options and variety are essential.

- They have a sense of destiny. They believe in their ability to make the world better and await leadership to ignite them to action.

Cultural Relevance

'Cultural relevance' was one of the buzz terms of the 1990s for churches seeking to reach a new generation of unchurched people. People are often interested in God and spiritual things, but many times the Church does not appeal to their interests or communicate in a manner that is comprehensible. To be effective in our mission, we must understand the attitudes, values and needs of the people in our community who we are trying to reach.[11] As every missionary knows, you cannot reach a people group anywhere without first understanding their culture.

There are many reasons why people won't come to church. Here are some of the major ones revealed in various surveys of the unchurched community:

- They don't think that church is relevant to their life.
- They don't like the music.
- They think the sermons are boring.
- They think that there's nothing for their children.
- They believe that people in churches tend to be 'holier than thou'.
- They think they will be pressured to give financially or to join the church.

We must be willing to break with unnecessary traditions and do away with anything that is in the way of reaching lost people for Christ. The greatest hindrance in reaching the unchurched is often the Church. The only thing that should offend a person coming to church should be the message of Christ crucified and even then, it should be presented as a message of hope. This isn't positive thinking. It is the good news.

Rick Warren says,

> 'Today's church is often stuck in forms of worship and ministry more appropriate to the nineteenth century. These can still be useful in targeting older people or those who have some religious heritage. However, because people under thirty with no church background comprise the largest percentage of the population, churches need to adopt a more contemporary cultural form of worship and ministry.'

We must adapt our ministry style to reach unchurched people not just to keep our current members happy (1 Corinthians 10:31–33). Too many churches are structured for the sake and comfort of those who are already Christians and are attending, rather than for the sake of those people who are unchurched. Church members assume that the church exists to meet their needs, therefore they structure their programs and facilities with that in mind. This is a fortress mentality.

God wants us to reach out beyond our walls to impact specific types of people groups in our communities. No church can reach everybody. People will attract and be attracted by those who are culturally similar to themselves. That's why it takes all kinds of churches to reach all kinds of people. Define your target group. What kind of people are you burdened to reach? What kind of people would respond to the style of your church and its leaders? Make a commitment before the Lord that you will work to fill your church with lost sheep (unchurched unbelievers) and stray sheep (unchurched believers), not just Christians who are already 'churched'.

Both Young and Old Together

Although there will be churches that target specific generations, I believe God's ideal is to have multi-generational churches. The young and the old need to work together for the cause of the kingdom, valuing their differences while appreciating their unique strengths. God wants to pour out His Spirit on both the young and the old. We need the wisdom of the aged and the energy of the young harnessed together for kingdom purpose.

Church leaders need to work hard at blending generations together in the ministry and focus of the Church. Here are some key attitudes of mutual respect to adopt.

- **The younger generation toward the older generation:**
  1. They need to honor and respect them.
  2. They need to be open to learn from them.
  3. They need to allow them to continue to contribute and serve.
  4. They need to seek to reach out to the growing older population and win them for Christ.

- **The older generation to the younger generation:**
  1. They need to love and respect them.
  2. They need to seek to be relevant to them.
  3. They need to pray for them, encourage them and teach them God's ways.
  4. They need to seek to reach out to those who don't know Christ.

Let's dwell together in a spirit of unity, understanding God's purposes for the generations.

I believe we must live with passion and watchfulness, as if Jesus may return today. We may be the last generation. However, we must also live with the wisdom and foresight that allows for the fact that we may not be the last generation and therefore, we must prepare the next generation to embrace the purposes of God.

It's time to make a **Generation Shift**. Are you passing the baton?

Notes

1. Wendell Smith's book, *Pastoring Youth in A New Generation*, further outlines these generation purposes (Portland, Oregon: Bible Temple Publishing, 1987).

2. This entire section on Satan's strategy and the Battlezones of Youth Culture has been adapted from Wendell Smith's *Dragon Slayer Seminar*. Wendell and his wife, Gini, pastor *The City Church* in Seattle, Washington.

3. This is from an article entitled *The Stolen Generation* published in the *Logos Journal*, November 1987.

4. Quoted from his book, *How to be a Hero to your Kids* (Dallas, Texas: Word Publishing, 1991, p .5).

5. From a sermon by Houston Miles, quoted by Stephen Strang in his article, *The Priority of Ministry to Kids*, in the March/April issue of *Ministries Today* (Strang Communications, p. 16).

6. These statistics are from an article by Robb Dunham, *How to Effectively Evangelise Children*, in the March/April issue of *Ministries Today* (Strang Communications, p. 42).

7. For an excellent analysis of the potential clash of generations within the Church and some practical solutions, see the book *The Three Generations* by Gary L. McIntosh (Tarrytown, New York: Fleming H. Revell, 1995).

8. Doug Murren's book, *The Baby Boomerang*, gives a very comprehensive overview of the Boomer generation and how the Church can reach them (Ventura, California: Regal Books, 1990).

9. For a very good book on reaching Busters, see *Inside the Soul of a New Generation* by T. Celek & D. Zander (Grand Rapids, Michigan: Zondervan Publishing House, 1996).

10. See Chapter 13 and 15 of this book for some excellent material about the critical role of music in the Church.

11. See Paul's philosophy of ministry in 1 Corinthians 9:19–23.

Personal Action Plan

Here are some ideas to help you make a personal **Generation Shift**:

1. Reach out to children and young people in your church. Take a personal interest in them and consider getting involved in this important ministry.
2. Reach out to elderly people in your church and help to make them feel special.
3. Have a tolerant attitude toward different generations and their styles or preferences. Try to understand people who are different from you and appreciate their uniqueness.
4. Think about the older people who have influenced your life positively. Write them a letter of thanks, buy them a gift or do something special for them to show your appreciation.
5. Be an example to younger people and seek to influence them for God.

Church Action Plan

Here are some ideas to help your church make a **Generation Shift**:

1. Put ample resources into building a vibrant ministry to children and young people.
2. Teach and train parents to raise godly children. Do this through regular preaching on the family, through seminars and through training courses.
3. Ensure that your leadership team has a balance of older and younger leaders.
4. Require every ministry leader to be raising up an assistant.
5. Think about the kind of people you want to reach and develop a church style that targets them specifically.
6. Develop a ministry or program for the older ones in your congregation. Encourage them to be involved in the ministry of the church and endeavor to make them feel valuable.
7. Honor the past. Have anniversary celebrations and thank those who have gone before and paved the way for today.
8. Teach about the history of the church and create an appreciation for the heroes of the past.
9. Teach about the importance and value of diversity.

Leading Your Church Through Change

It's time to advance and move forward in God (Deuteronomy 1:6–8; 2:3). We must move out of the old and make the transition into the new. Human nature wants to go back to the way we always did things and the security of the past. A leader's role is to motivate people to move forward into God's purposes.

God is a God who never changes but He requires us to be continually changing. Paul tells us that God is transforming us from one degree of glory to another by the Holy Spirit (2 Corinthians 3:18). The Christian life is to be a life of growth and growth means constant change.

We need to be anchored to the Rock, the unmovable **principles** of Scriptures, yet moving with the times by being willing to change our **methods**.

You Are Called to Be a Change Agent

As church leaders, God wants us to **lead** change, not just manage it, cope with it or understand it. We are to initiate change by moving God's people forward to where they need to be.

This implies an awareness of four things:

1. Where you've come from (heritage and roots) – the **past**. We are to build on the past without worshipping it.

2. Where you are now (insight) – the **present**. How are we doing? What is the present reality?

3. Where you should be (vision) – the **future**. What could God do through us?

4. The steps needed to get there (strategy) – the **process**. How will we make it a reality?

The prophetic dimension helps you tap into God's eternal purposes and His thoughts about your part in particular. The apostolic dimension provides you with the wisdom, authority and courage to initiate appropriate changes.

Different Types of Leaders

Like any gift, the leadership gift can be expressed in a wide variety of styles and approaches. George Barna, in his book, *The Second Coming of the Church*, shares four different leadership styles.[1]

1. **A directing leader.** This kind of leader is a visionary force who sees the big picture and motivates people with great passion. They are full of ideas but may have difficulty working out the details of how it will happen.

2. **A strategic leader.** This kind of leader has high analytical abilities and is able to wisely plan and put information into logical order. Sometimes this kind of person may tend towards perfectionism and may lack people skills.

3. **A team-building leader.** This kind of leader is able to communicate really well and has the ability to develop good relationships with others. Because of this they are able to mobilize people effectively. Their weakness may be that they become too emotionally involved with people and they may lose sight of the big picture.

4. **An operational leader.** This kind of leader is good at management, structure, organization and creating efficiency. Their weakness can sometimes be that they are too cautious or that they fail to have long term vision.

It is very rare to find a leader who has a balance of all these styles. That is why it is best if leaders work closely together with a leadership team of people with multiple and varied gifts.

Preparing for Change

Before we look at some principles for leading change, let's note some important prerequisite qualities in the leader God calls to be a **change agent**:

1. Leading change takes tremendous **courage**, confidence and security. It will not be easy. You must know that you have been called of God and that the change is being initiated by Him.

2. Leading change requires much **wisdom**. Decisions will have to be made and problems will have to be solved.

3. Leading change requires trust, rapport and **credibility** with the people involved.

4. Leading change requires a genuine **love** for people. We are called to lead strongly, confidently and with boldness but never through the use of threats, manipulation or intimidation.

    Remember that for change to work, **people** must change. Focus on the people involved and not just the mechanics of the change. People are the 'gatekeepers of change' and they ultimately determine whether change is successful or not. Build strong healthy relationships and keep close to people as you manage the change.

5. Leading change requires a 'win/win' mentality. Positive change should benefit everyone involved.

6. Leading change requires an understanding that change is a **process** and it takes time. Every change involves an ending, a transition, and then a new beginning.[2]

7. Leading change requires **patience**. Don't try to go too fast and don't get frustrated or impatient along the way. Change has to take place over a long period of time. It will take a number of years to reshape your ministry.

8. Leading change requires that you change too. We lead by **example** and therefore we must model the change personally. Be a change agent. Leadership is the key. Leaders resist change as much as followers do. You must be the first to change.

Principles for Leading Change

Each one of the seven **Strategic Shifts** we have looked at needs to take place in the church. Unless you keep changing and growing, your church will plateau and decline. It will take wise, godly leaders to make the appropriate and necessary changes so the church remains relevant and effective in the twenty-first century.

Unfortunately, churches tend to resist change and have little or no mechanism for working their way through change. We all hear a lot of good things, but we often do very little about it. Reading this book will only help you if you are willing to do something about it.

Let's look at a man named Nehemiah who successfully led some significant change in his time and see what we can learn from him to help us as we lead change in the church.

Here are eight principles for leading change.

1. See the need for change

Nehemiah was working in a comfortable job in the palace of a foreign king. He received a report from his homeland, Israel, about the terrible condition of his people and their capital city, Jerusalem. His heart was moved. A burden came upon him. Something had to happen. Things had to change. The current condition was a disgrace to God and His people (Nehemiah 1:1–4; 2:3).

All positive change begins with seeing the need for it first. If we are willing to ask ourselves the tough questions and realistically look at our current situation, we can't help but see the need for change. So often we become comfortable and seemingly immune to the desperate problems and challenges around about us.

Every problem presents an opportunity for God to move and for the Church to express His love and compassion.

Get out on the street and look at our world, then look at the Church. Spend time in prayer and allow God to move your emotions. He will use sorrow, grief, compassion and even anger to motivate you to do something to make things different.

Change for change's sake is crazy, but change aimed at helping people and improving things is essential. Leaders are change agents and they constantly see the need for further change in order to accomplish God's purposes and plans.

Build all change upon the principles of God's Word. God's Word gives people security. Tie everything you do into the unshakeable and unchanging principles of God's Word. As we lead according to God's direction, we can be sure we have His support and backing.

The Church needs to change and be transformed! We need to become more relevant and more impacting as we seek to reach more people for Christ.

2. Receive a clear vision from God

Nehemiah spent time in prayer and waiting on God. God showed him that he was to rebuild the walls of the city of Jerusalem (Nehemiah 1:5–11; 2:5). It was a big task, but it had to be done.

All vision begins with seeing the big picture of what God wants to do. As we spend time in prayer, God will show us what He can do through us and give us a vision of a preferred future.

Every Christian and every leader needs to invest time into receiving a clear vision from God for their life and ministry. There is a big difference between **vision** and **ambition**. Ambition is what I want for my life. Vision is what God wants for my life.

Effective leaders tie all change to vision and purpose. They know where they're headed and why.

3. Create a strategic plan

Nehemiah knew exactly what God wanted him to do (vision) and he had thought through all the details of how he would do it (strategy). When asked by the king what he wanted, he was able to answer clearly and precisely. When asked how long it would take, he knew the exact time frame and he was also able to list the specific resources he would need to accomplish his task (Nehemiah 2:6–9).

He had obviously put a lot of time and effort into thinking

through and developing a strategic plan to make the vision a reality.

Once Nehemiah arrived in Jerusalem with the blessing of the king, he did further personal research to help him fine-tune his strategy (Nehemiah 2:11–16). He went and observed the actual areas that needed change. He didn't just come up with some plan to solve an imaginary problem.

Accurate information is essential before you start making changes. As leaders, we must 'know' and be fully aware of the state of our congregation (Proverbs 27:23) and then we must give attention to making positive change. Get involved at the 'grass roots' level of the church and your local community. Observe, ask questions and listen really well. Take surveys, if necessary, and catch the pulse of the people.

Unfortunately, many church leaders don't take time to plan like Nehemiah did. This needs to change because God is a planner. He had a plan in creation as He formed the world. He broke this task down into six bite-sized days of work. Then He rested on the last day of the week. Everything was done according to plan and within the estimated time frame. God also has a plan for redemption and He is working to accomplish it.

God gives visions to men and women and requires them to think and plan ahead. God gave Joseph a 14-year plan (Genesis 41:25–57). That's a **long**-term forecast!

Wise leaders take their God-given vision and form it into a plan that describes how and when the vision will become a reality. This takes time and involves a process. It needs wise and godly counsel from other leaders. The more significant the change, the more necessary it is to have the input from all perspectives.

4. Speak to the influencers

The first thing Nehemiah did was to speak to the king. Without his blessing, the task would not even get underway (Nehemiah 2:3–6).

The next thing Nehemiah did was to go and talk to the Elders of Israel in the city of Jerusalem (Nehemiah 2:16–18). He did not go straight to the people and he did not begin working himself. He realized that unless those who were in positions of influence bought into the vision, the change would not occur.

When speaking to the Elders, he did not present the solution first. He actually spoke to them about the problem so that they would agree on the need for change. Notice what he said.

> *'You see the trouble we are in: Jerusalem lies in ruins, and its gates have been burned with fire. Come, let us rebuild the wall of Jerusalem, and we will no longer be in disgrace.'*
> (Nehemiah 2:17)

Unless people see and embrace the need for change, they will not be willing to pay the price, or be committed to the work required to bring the change about. People need to understand the purpose of the change and see the benefits it will bring.

Wisdom teaches us that all change needs to be communicated and directed through the proper leadership channels and structures. We must influence the influencers. Seek to understand the change process and the proper channels of authority and accountability. Work with this, not around it. Only when the key influencers are in unity can change occur without unnecessary damage.

When people see the need for change and catch a realistic vision of how things could be better, they become motivated to be a part of the solution.

5. Organize the work to be done

Now Nehemiah was ready to put the people to work. He knew things had to change. He had a vision with a strategic plan and the influencers were in total agreement.

His next step was to break the work down into specific tasks and then delegate it to the people. He mobilized everyone into working teams and then gave each group specific objectives. Nehemiah placed over forty groups of people at different places along the wall each with a unique task but all working together for a common vision (Nehemiah 3:1–32).

A church leader must seek to acquire ownership from the

entire congregation for positive change to take place. It needs to become their vision so that they are committed enough to work towards it.

6. Deal with the opposing forces

I wish I could tell you that there will be no problems when you lead change, but the reality is that movement causes friction. Resistance to change is normal and so we need to prepare for it and handle it wisely.

Nehemiah faced external opposition from those who were against the change. This opposition intensified as more and more progress was made (Nehemiah 2:10, 19–20; 4:1–3, 7–8, 11–12; 6:1–14). It started with mild dislike and ended with outright aggressive attack. In the same way, you will know what it is to face the onslaught of the enemy whenever you try to bring about positive change in the Church. The devil hates the Church and he especially targets churches that are a threat to his kingdom of darkness. You can be sure that you will experience spiritual warfare if you are advancing and taking ground for God.

Nehemiah countered this external attack with prayer (Nehemiah 4:4–5). He kept the people alert, awake and ready for battle at all times (Nehemiah 4:13–14, 16–23; 5:9, 19). His confidence was in God and he refused to be intimidated (Nehemiah 2:20).

In addition to the external attack, Nehemiah also encountered internal problems along the way.

The first internal problem was discouragement. They were half way done on the project and the people felt like giving up (Nehemiah 4:6, 10). You can hear them saying things such as, 'Is it worth it?', 'Is it really possible?' and 'Whose idea was this anyway?' Nehemiah had to lift their morale and encourage them to finish the work that they had started. He reminded them that God was with them and that their very future was at stake (Nehemiah 4:14).

Any change in the church starts out with a lot of enthusiasm, at least in those who initiated the change. But change is a process and it doesn't always happen as quickly and as smoothly as we'd like it to. It's easy to get discouraged along the way and feel like giving up. However, we must remember the urgent need for the change and embrace the vision God has given us once again.

The next internal problem Nehemiah faced was conflict (Nehemiah 5:1–13). He immediately went to work bringing resolution to the situation. This required getting all of the facts by listening to everyone involved in the conflict. Notice the different stories that were being given by the different groups of people (Nehemiah 5:1–5). Nehemiah was very angry, but he first pondered everything carefully, then confronted in love (Nehemiah 5:6–7).

As we lead change, there may be conflicts that emerge. It is vital that we resolve them quickly and thoroughly. Don't ignore them! Get all the facts and never confront when you're angry. We must learn the balance of having the **courage** to confront the issues and the **consideration** to do it in a loving manner (Ephesians 4:15; 2 Timothy 2:24–26).

Nehemiah led with a servant spirit and with an integrity of heart that gave him great credibility with the people (Nehemiah 5:14–19). Because he was able to resolve the conflicts, the work went on. If he had not resolved these issues, the fulfillment of the vision would have been aborted.

In every change, there will be opposing forces. Someone or something will face loss, despite the many gains. As mentioned earlier, letting go of the old can be extremely difficult and until people have taken hold of the new, the 'in-between' time can be similar to the sensation a trapeze artist must feel as he hangs in mid-air, reaching to take hold of the bar. You may encounter anger, frustration, fear, uncertainty and disappointment during the transition. Wise leaders think through the possible reactions or problems and avoid unnecessary conflict by preparing for and addressing these forces in advance.

7. Communicate continually

Throughout the entire project, Nehemiah stayed close to the people and to the progress of the project. He was always listening and observing how things were going (Nehemiah 4:14, 19–20, 22; 5:1–19; 6:1–19). Based on his observations, he made adjustments and further fine-tuned his strategy while keeping focused on the overall vision. He continually communicated with the people, encouraging them and giving them direction.

When leading change, we must stay close to the change process and actively **lead** the transition from the old to the new. People need to be constantly inspired and motivated about the importance of the vision and the progress that is being made.

We all tend to drift and vision can easily become blurred. Wise leaders constantly bring the vision back into focus and never allow people to be satisfied with the way things are.

Announcing a change or coming up with a vision statement is the easy part of leading change. It's harder to then translate that vision into a workable plan. But it's even more difficult to implement that plan step by step and monitor it until it is completed. This takes diligence, patience and focused attention.

8. Don't give up

Nehemiah led the people of Israel to finish the work in exactly fifty-two days (Nehemiah 6:15–16)! He saw the need for change, then received a clear vision from God. He translated that vision into a strategic plan, brought all the influencers into agreement, then mobilized the people to work. He dealt with the opposing internal forces along the way by continual communication. But best of all, he did not quit when the going got tough. He worked hard and he refused to give up. Eventually, he finished! He was a man with a vision who made it a reality.

Oh, the joy and fulfillment that comes when you are able to bring about positive change. It requires God's help and a lot of patient endurance on the part of the leader.

Don't give up. Persevere. If the vision is from God, it's worth fighting for. Don't chop and change direction. Yes, make adjustments along the way, but finish what you start. Commit to it and be willing to pay the price.

Creating Positive Change

In Luke 5:36–39, Jesus told this interesting parable:

'*No one tears a patch from a new garment and sews it on an old one. If he does, he will have torn the new garment, and the patch from the new will not match the old. And no one pours new wine into old wineskins. If he does, the new wine will burst the skins, the wine will run out and the wineskins will be ruined. No, new wine must be poured into new wineskins. And no one after drinking old wine wants the new, for he says, "The old is better." '*

Every church has its old members (not necessarily in age!) who are used to the old wine and think the old way of doing things is better. They were probably in the church **before** the changes were made and they may find it difficult to adjust to the new way of doing things. This is natural as all change takes time to process.

The new ones who have come in **after** the change usually love the new because that's all they know.

The challenge is to continue to provide new wine and wean those old ones on to it. Even Jesus said, 'No one, having drunk old wine, **immediately** desires new; for he says, "The old is better." ' In the process, mixing in a little old wine may be wise. Jesus also said,

'*Therefore every scribe instructed concerning the kingdom of heaven is like a householder who brings out of his treasure things **new and old**.'* (Matthew 13:52, NKJV)

Making sudden, radical or **revolutionary** change, although sometimes necessary, will usually cause a reaction. Gradual **evolutionary** change often works much better as it enables people to adjust over a period of time.[3]

Different people respond differently to change. Innovators and dreamers love change and seek to constantly create it. Other people know a good idea when they see it and embrace the change once they are given time to understand it. Some people naturally tend to be more hesitant and skeptical. Don't rebuke them. Take time to talk with them and hear their concerns. Often, you will gain further insight from them into how to make the change more successful and you will give them the chance to hear your heart and the motivation for the change.

Some may or will not change. Once you turn the church, which may be likened to a bus, in a new direction or on a different route, some people will inevitably get off to join another bus going in a direction they want to go. You have to be prepared for this, although keeping as many with you as possible is the aim!

I think the most challenging task of leadership is to manage change and transition. The key issue is knowing in your own spirit that God is leading you and that you are moving out in His will for your ministry and your church. The giants will be there and the need for courage will be great, but God will not fail you or let you fail. As you seek Him, He will guide you, give you wisdom and favor with the people.

Change is not easy, in fact, it can be very uncomfortable. However, the Church must change and be transformed if it is to be what God intends it to be in the world.

Notes

1. Dallas, Texas: Word Publishing, 1998, pp. 114–118.

2. The book *Managing Transitions*, by William Bridges, has some very good material on helping people through times of change and transition (Reading, Massachusetts: Addison-Wesley Publishing, 1991).

3. For some excellent material on leading change and why people tend to resist it, see Chapter 4 of John Maxwell's book *Developing the Leader Within You* (Nashville, Tennessee: Thomas Nelson Publishing, 1993).

Personal Action Plan

Here are some questions and ideas to help you be a part of leading change in your church:

1. Why do you think change so hard?
2. What are some of the dangers during times of change?
3. What things can you do to assist your church in the area of change?
4. How can you encourage people that you know to be more willing to change?
5. What are some keys to change being successful?
6. How do you respond personally to change?
7. Read the **Church Action Plan** and do the exercise for yourself.

Church Action Plan

Here are some ideas to help you lead your church through change:

1. Rate your church or ministry from a 1–10 on each **Strategic Shift** (1 being the lowest and 10 being the highest).
2. What are your lowest two scores?
3. Do something about improving these areas in the next three months. Gather resources to help you. You may even want to seek external help or advice from someone who is strong in your areas of weakness.
4. Keep evaluating and making necessary adjustments by doing this exercise throughout the year.
5. What are your highest two scores? Seek to be of assistance to other people or churches in the area of your strengths.

Conclusion

We began by talking about the fact that the Church is God's master project. As you can see, there is much to be done and it will take a lot of work. But God is for us and He has given us all the resources we need to accomplish the task.

The best news is that once God begins something, He always finishes it. He never leaves things half done or decides midway through to give up. He has begun a good work and he will complete it!

Back to the Future

The seven **Strategic Shifts** we have shared in this book are actually a return to the basic principles of the New Testament churches. God has ordained these shifts. They return us to biblical Christianity operating in the context of our generation and culture. We must discern them, embrace them and lead our people forward wisely, yet boldly.

If the Church wants to be relevant and impacting in our generation, then it must embrace the original blueprint given by God to the first Church in the book of Acts.

The early Church was a Church of:

1. Fervent prayer.

2. Passionate outreach.

3. Loving relationships.

4. Empowering leaders.

5. Mobilized believers.

6. United communities.

7. Generational baton passing.

As we embrace these shifts, I believe the world will see a demonstration of the dynamic power and love of God through the Church of Jesus Christ.

That's what I'm giving my life for. What about you? Help tranform your church!

If you have enjoyed this book and would like to help us to
send a copy of it and many other titles to needy pastors in
the **Third World**, please write for further information
or send your gift to:

**Sovereign World Trust
PO Box 777, Tonbridge
Kent TN11 0ZS
United Kingdom**

or to the '**Sovereign World**' distributor in your country.

Visit our website at **www.sovereign-world.org**
for a full range of Sovereign World books.